It Just Wasn't Perfect For Me

It Just Wasn't Perfect For Me

Perfect For Me

My 50 Years in Television and Radio Broadcasting

RICK D'AMICO

ISBN: 1539786994
ISBN-13: 9781539786993
Library of Congress Control Number: 2016918273
CreateSpace Independent Publishing Platform
North Charleston, South Carolina

CONTENTS

PREFACE

When you get old, you have a lot of stories to tell. During my career in the ever-young business of broadcasting, I got to work with wide-eyed kids graduating from college who always asked the same questions: Are people as crazy at other stations as they are here? Is this business worth the sacrifice of trying to stay in it? I tell them my stories of the bizarre things that happened as I worked my way up in radio and TV. Most of my listeners are flabbergasted. They almost always say, "You should write a book!" Well, here it is.

I've mentioned this book a number of times on Facebook and Twitter and in broadcasts when I was on the air, and I always got the same question: "When's it coming out?"

I usually responded by saying, "Never—it's the book that will never get published!" After all, who would be interested in stories about a simple guy trying to earn a living in broadcasting?

However, motivational speakers, professional trainers, and college students have asked me any number of times to write a book about what it *really* takes to succeed in television and radio broadcasting. They've complained, "Colleges and universities teach the academic side of the trade, but what is it really like to butt heads against corporate bigwigs; mean news directors; incompetent producers; and silly, small-town station managers, and in some cases, to face bigotry and racism? What's it like to start at the very bottom and claw your way up, facing disappointment and setback after setback?"

Whether you're reading this because you want to be in broadcasting or you're already in it and want to advance your career, I hope this book is an eye-opener. And if you watched TV news in Phoenix (or any TV news show) or are a fan of radio and have wondered what goes on behind the scenes, you'll probably get a kick out of this book.

You'll hear the real reason owners and managers run radio and television stations. Is it to serve the public, inform, and entertain? Come on!

So what does it really take to be successful as an on-air performer? College? Academics? *Really?* Then why did a news anchor with whom I worked, who had a master's degree in journalism from Northwestern University, hide under the anchor desk when she didn't have a script to read?

In order to be successful, you have to press on, and in order to press on, you have to have this one thing I describe throughout the book. If you don't have it, you'll never make it!

You'll learn why many people in broadcasting management hate those who perform on the air. (Or, at least, they just don't get them and get IT!)

I also want to show you how I discovered my real purpose in life and by doing this perhaps, help steer you in the right direction toward your career goals.

I also will reveal the one secret nearly all on-air performers have. One of the nation's great network-news anchors revealed this on his last day on the air. It's a secret we all share.

This is not a textbook! It's a true-to-life story, as I remember it, of what really happened to me. I had to change some names and leave others out so as not to embarrass people and, really, just to be nice.

And more than anything else, this book is meant to be entertaining and fun. When I told these stories to my fellow broadcasters over the years, they always responded, "That's unbelievable, bizarre, and/or hilarious; that never could have happened!" Well, it did. It's all true—the good; the bad; and, most of all, the fun!

So here it is. This is my story.

—Rick D'Amico

INTRODUCTION

There are many reasons I should not have been successful in broadcasting: I had no formal training. I never went to college. I was raised by a single parent (my father died when I was twelve). And most of all, at the beginning of my career, my voice was so high and scratchy that a lot of stations told me to get lost! Or, more politely, they just said they had no openings for me.

I used to keep a box with all the rejection letters I received from radio and television stations all over the country. It was a very large box! But there were a few "miracles," as I like to think of them, that happened along the way and turned things around, leading me to what I like to think was success and a wonderful career in television news. As boxing champion Rocky Graziano said in the title of his autobiography, *Somebody Up There Likes Me!*

I was twelve years old when my father died, and it was such a shock— the most traumatic event in my life. I found myself spending most of my time alone in my bedroom, just listening to the radio. At the time, there were such radio personalities on the air in Cleveland, Ohio, as Alan "Moon Dog" Freed, who coined the term "rock and roll." Others were Bill Randall, Phil McLean, Casey Kasem, Soupy Sales, and later Pete Myers and Johnny Holliday—radio people I idolized.

Every night, after listening to these radio greats, I would get down on my knees next to my bed and pray, "Lord, please let me have a career in radio and television broadcasting. Please work a miracle in my life and give me a shot—I just want a chance!"

■ ■ ■

So how did I come up with the title of my book? On a very hot summer day in Phoenix, Arizona, my granddaughter, who at the time was three years old, was advancing in her swimming class.

She was very excited. After she'd spent a few weeks in beginner's group number one, her instructor told her, "You are going into intermediate group number two, because you are such a good swimmer!" My granddaughter was ecstatic.

We knew she had a lot of friends in group one and that group two would be a little more difficult, but she was eager and ready. My wife and I held her hands and walked her over to group two. She jumped in the water, the instructor took over, and we went to find a Coke and some shade.

Just a few minutes later, we went back to watch her swim, and she was gone! She was nowhere to be seen! My wife and I panicked: "Oh my God, where is she?" She could have drowned; it's happened before when instructors lose sight of a student. We searched, but our granddaughter didn't appear. I got the idea to walk back over to group one. And there she was, swimming with her friends!

I pulled her out of the pool and asked, "Why did you leave group two to go back to group one?"

She answered, "Because, Papa, *it just wasn't perfect for me!*"

When I told my coanchors this story, they said this would be a wonderful title for my book.

As you read, you'll discover why!

1

DEEP IN THE HEART OF DIXIE: JOHNNY REB RADIO

*We got out of the car, and he pulled the gun out of his holster. It was pitch-black outside; we were alone in a swamp in Georgia, and he had a gun. I was thinking, **They'll never find my body out here!***

I waited outside the barracks for the cab to arrive. It was a cold Easter Sunday morning in Albany, Georgia, on April 14, 1963.

I was so excited and nervous I could hardly contain myself. I was on my way to my very first broadcasting job! This was the first time I would be on the air, all by myself, and get paid as a disc jockey and radio announcer.

The cab pulled up, I got in, and the driver said in a very thick Georgian drawl, "Where y'all going to?"

I was so excited to say, "Johnny Reb Radio!"

"That's in the Holiday Inn?" he said.

"That's right," I replied.

The cabbie knew the radio station was in the Holiday Inn because every hour on the hour and on the half hour, the station ran a jingle and an announcement that said it was in the Holiday Inn. It was certainly a trade-out agreement, whereby the station didn't have to pay rent.

The journey into town from Turner Air Force Base, where I was stationed while serving in the US Air Force, took about a half hour. I had joined the air force hoping to be in Armed Forces Radio, but instead they had made me a hospital administrator. So I had to get my radio career started another way, and somehow I had landed this cool part-time job.

I sat in the back of the cab and thought about how I loved radio; about how, as a child of twelve years old growing up in Cleveland, Ohio, I had found solace in listening to the radio; and about the gargantuan talents who had been on the air in Cleveland at the time.

Still in the cab, I dreamed of working at the same stations as these legends. I was so excited to be in this glamorous business; I was on my way to radio heaven.

The cab pulled up to the Holiday Inn, and as I stepped out, I noticed something peculiar: the lights were on in the glass-enclosed studio upstairs.

Johnny Reb Radio was WALG-AM 1590, a Top 40 rock-and-roll station. Its studios were somewhat of a landmark in Albany, Georgia—not really in the Holiday Inn, but on the property out in front with two large glass-enclosed, second-story studios looking down over the city. As people drove by, many would beep their horn in approval of a record on the air at the time…or perhaps just to say hello.

But, on this early morning, why were the lights on? You see, in those days many radio stations did not broadcast twenty-four hours a day. Johnny Reb signed off at midnight and back on at 6:00 a.m.

I was the Sunday-morning sign-on jock. It was an entry-level position—you get there, turn on the lights, turn on the equipment, turn on the transmitter, and then play music in between the church services that were either broadcast live or on tape.

So there I was, just beginning my career and hoping to follow in the footsteps of the famous DJs of my dreams, but when I walked up the stairs to the studio that day, I knew I had a problem: someone was already inside! I thought, *Oh my God, we're being robbed!*

I walked into the control room (the studio where DJs play the music), and I was shocked to see a guy wearing a straw hat, like one Frank Sinatra might wear; casual clothes; and a pistol in a holster on his side. A gun! Now I thought for sure that we were being robbed!

In the midst of the wires all over the place, with both feet up on the radio-control board, he was talking on the phone. He hung up and looked over to me. "You the sign-on jock?"

"Yes."

"I'm the chief engineer. We're off the air—can't get the transmitter to work."

He tried to explain the problem as broadcast engineers often do, in terms and words that are beyond the average person's comprehension and certainly beyond that of someone just starting out in the business.

He said, "You want to come with me to get this fixed?"

"Sure," I replied, thinking I wanted to be on the air as soon as possible. We drove to the transmitter site, which was out in a Georgia swamp. When we got out of the car, he pulled the gun out of his holster. It was pitch-black outside; we were alone in a swamp in Georgia, and he had a gun. I was thinking, *They'll never find my body out here!*

"Ah...what do you need that for?" I was a little apprehensive.

"Gators and snakes, son," he said nonchalantly. He told me he had shot many an alligator and cottonmouth rattler on those wood boards leading up to the transmitter building. So then I went from being apprehensive to shaking in my boots.

My eyes bulged out of my skull as we balanced ourselves on two wooden planks to walk through the swamp up to the door of a filthy transmitter shack. The inside looked like a scene from an Indiana Jones movie; it was a mess, with wires hanging all over the place, dirt everywhere, and huge panels of equipment with glowing tubes. And there was actually a dead snake on the floor! The chief engineer checked the equipment and didn't find anything wrong. I was more concerned about the gators and snakes, but none were to be seen, and we drove off to the telephone company downtown, where the audio and control lines went through on their way to the transmitter.

I'll never forget what happened there. A telephone technician, a good ol' big Georgia boy working the overnight shift, showed us how the lines between the radio station and the transmitter were working fine. Then he showed us the special communications hotline that came in from Offutt Air Force Base, in Omaha, Nebraska, headquarters of the US Air Force Strategic Air Command, and went to Turner Air Force Base. He said, "All you have to do is throw this switch, and the line goes dead, and a warning horn sounds!"

I thought, *Holy cow, some guy working the overnight shift in the phone company in Georgia can disrupt the operations of the Strategic Air Command and the B-52 bombers that fly day and night to protect our country? Who is this guy?* Who knows? But this was 1963, during the Cold War. Judged by post-9/11 standards, this situation would be an outrage.

After we arrived back at the studio, it took about three hours for the chief engineer to get the station on the air.

Finally, I got to go on the air! I was starting my dream! I played a jingle: "Johnny Reb RAID—EEE—OOOO..." The jingle was rocking, and I opened the mike and said, "Good morning, and Happy Easter. I'm D'Amico [the program director thought it would be cool if I used only one name, like Annette or Cher or something. Who was I to argue—it was my first job!]. Let me entertain you now on jumping Johnny Reb!" Then I played a record.

I guess I should explain here. Radio in those days was much different from how it is today. Back then, we played records—those shiny, round, flat, black things, made of plastic with grooves in them, which contained the sound. We placed the records on a turntable, or record player, which we generally had two of in our studios. And then we put the needle on the record. The needle had a long arm on it, with a wire that picked up the sound from the groove and sent it out somewhere to be broadcast. Also, we placed tiny reels of recording tape on tape recorders that had commercials and radio jingles on them. The DJ did all this manually.

As soon as that record started, a big red light in the studio started flashing; the phone—that is, the station's private line, the hotline—was ringing. Only bosses called on this line.

"Hello," I said.

"It's Mark Schorr, general manager," the voice on the other end said. "Listen, I want you to go back on the air and play every commercial we missed when we were off the air. I don't care if you play them back-to-back, one after another, as long as you play them all; do you understand?"

I said, "Should I play some records in between?"

"No, no, just play the spots. I don't care what else you do, but play the spots. Get them all in. Do you understand? Play the spots! Play the commercials! *Play the spots!*" he said desperately.

As I've mentioned, the station had been off the air for about three hours. Did the station manager care that we might have lost our audience? No. Did he care that people who were depending on the station for news, weather information, and entertainment would not be served? No. Did he care that if we played commercials for more than an hour, it would not do the advertisers—the people who were paying for those very same commercials—much good, because who would listen to an hour of commercials? No.

All he cared about was playing the commercials so he could get the advertisers' money!

This was my introduction to the next fifty-plus years of my career life: Broadcasting is a business; all owners and managers really want to do is to make money. Whether they make it by playing rock and roll (all the management and owners I worked for in those early days of rock and roll hated it, but they played it because it was profitable) or by being a conservative talk station, they broadcast because they make money doing it. It's all about making money—profit.

But playing all the spots one after another wasn't easy. All the commercials were on little tape spools, and they had to be cued up individually on one of two tape recorders in the studio. I sat there for what seemed like an hour, playing one commercial after another. Every now and then, I would throw in a Johnny Reb jingle, then play more spots.

This hour seemed like a lifetime. When I got them all in, the general manager must have been ecstatic; the very last commercial played just in time for the beginning of the "Sunday Morning with Tennessee Ernie Ford Gospel Hour Show"!

After this, my shift was over. Well, so much for my stardom and the glamorous career of radio broadcasting!

And little did I know at that early stage that my brand-new career was about to be cut extremely short.

2

WELCOME TO RADIO; YOU'RE FIRED!

**In Albany, Georgia, in the early sixties, I should
have known there were separate restrooms and
"colored-only" water fountains...**

Working at Johnny Reb Radio was frightening and exciting at the same time.

Let me explain: I was new to this. And really, anything new is exciting. Also, this was my dream, and I got the biggest kick out of people knowing I was on the radio. It was a real thrill.

I remember going into the station to work on Saturday afternoons, thinking the whole city was listening to me—how cool. But I also remember the times I sat in the studio waiting to announce a record or come out of a record while I was so scared I couldn't talk! I would shake; I actually had mike fright.

Also, I had this tremendous fear that I would let a record run out, and there would be nothing on the air—silence, or as we called it, dead air. To this day, I still have nightmares that I'm in a radio studio and the record ends while I'm not paying attention.

But what I really had to fear in my first radio job was something I never would have thought of in a million years—something I believe led to my being fired!

The year was 1963, and I was nineteen years old. I was born and raised in Cleveland, Ohio. When I arrived at Turner Air Force Base in Albany, Georgia, I immediately noticed the strange behavior of other people who were from the Deep South.

As I went through the cafeteria line in the air force dining hall, for example, the cooks would say something like, "Hey da', meek-ee-o, how 'bout some Mexican hot sauce for your taters? That's right up your alley, ain't it, boy?"

(I thought, *These people are so stupid; they don't even know I'm Italian!*)

Because of this behavior, I normally gravitated to people who were like me: guys from the big urban areas up north, such as New York and Chicago. And many of them were African Americans.

We'd drink beer in the barracks at night and listen to rhythm-and-blues music on radio stations out of Nashville and Memphis. We dressed alike and many times just hung out together.

One day, a sergeant supervisor came into our work area and said the hospital in town needed people to give blood, and volunteers got the day off. My good friend David Fitzpatrick and I volunteered. Fitzpatrick was African American, from New York City. We went into town together.

David and I walked side by side through town, and at first I couldn't figure it out: Why were people staring at me? Why were people giving me the most disgusted looks I had ever seen?

We gave blood at the hospital and then stopped in at a lunch counter to have a hamburger and a Coke. Did I mention the year was 1963? Did I mention this was Albany, Georgia?

The clerk at the counter looked at me and said, "We don't serve him, and we ain't serving you!" Everyone in the place stared; some even got up and gathered around us.

David and I were shocked. We looked at each other and started laughing, really laughing out loud, and got up and left. I was from Cleveland,

Ohio, and David was from New York City, so neither of us had experienced anything like this before. We sat together on the military bus back to the base, then got a beer and hamburger at the airmen's service club.

In Albany, Georgia, in the early sixties, I should have known there were separate restrooms and "colored-only" water fountains; white people with hatred in their eyes would glare at you when you walked down the street with a fellow black soldier, airman, or marine who was helping to keep our nation safe during the Cold War. This was unbelievable to a kid who had grown up north of the Mason-Dixon Line.

Now think about this. I was working at Johnny Reb Radio, a station named after the epitome of a Confederate soldier. The station used to play the rebel yell—a sound effect of Johnny Reb screaming—throughout the day between records. When radio stations across the nation signed on and off for the day, they played the national anthem. But not Johnny Reb Radio; it played "Dixie," the rocking Duane Eddy version.

The story of how I got the job there was somewhat bizarre and also fairly telling about my future profession. One Saturday morning, I had worked up enough nerve to take the bus downtown and walk into the radio station out of the blue. I said I wanted to be a DJ there. The first program director I talked to told me to come back in a week...but when I returned, he'd been fired! Another employee told me to come back another week after that.

The second time I returned, the new program director hadn't arrived yet.

When I returned a third time, I met the new program director, who had just been fired from a big radio station in Atlanta, WQXI, known down south as "Qxie in Dixie." His name was Shannon. That's the name he used on the air, one name—just as he wanted me to do. He took me under his wing and trained me. I learned a lot about radio from Shannon; I really don't know why he took me on to mentor, but it was a lucky break for me and surely an answer to my prayers.

When he thought I was ready, Shannon set me free, to be by myself doing the Sunday morning sign-on shift.

"Now listen," he said. "Don't get too raucous. Your shift is on Sunday morning, so play softer music, and we have some church services and religious shows too."

"I can bring some of my records in and play them?" I said in a sort-of question.

"Sure, no problem...just softer stuff, nothing hard."

So I brought in some of my albums. Have I mentioned that I really love music by black artists? I played songs by the Platters, Dina Washington, Nancy Wilson, Ray Charles (who, by the way, was born in Albany, Georgia), and Sam Cooke, to name a few. Did I mention the year was 1963? Did I mention this was Albany, Georgia?

About a month later, while I was on the air, a large man came walking into the studio. He was dressed in a white suit and white hat—the works, like someone out of an Orson Welles movie.

"Can I help you?" I asked. He looked at me with astonishment and disgust and didn't answer.

He was talking with some lackey he came with about something and paid no attention to me. I said, "How'd you guys get in the building?" The man looked as if he'd be lowering his standards by talking to me, and he walked out of the studio.

Turns out he was the son of the station owner, who also owned other Johnny Reb stations across Georgia.

The following Monday, I got a call from the general manager, Mark Schor. "Rick, can you come in? I need to talk to you."

He told me they were cutting part-timers from the budget and would have to let me go.

Now, here's the fun part. I had never gotten paid to begin with! They had said they would pay me when my training was over. My salary was to be $1.09 an hour.

So why was I fired? Playing black music on a Sunday morning on a station called Johnny Reb Radio, in Albany, Georgia, in 1963 might have had something to do with it. (Johnny Reb was a Top 40 station, but it very seldom played music by black artists.)

A couple of months later, Martin Luther King Jr. (whose family, by the way, sponsored a show on my Sunday morning shift, "King and King Insurance Gospel Hour") led the march on Washington, DC, and made his famous "I Have a Dream" speech.

3

OUT ON THE FARM IN ASHTABULA

Now I was thinking he was going to ask me to
clean out the bathrooms!

To say WREO Radio in Ashtabula, Ohio, was in a rural area is an understatement.

I was fresh out of the air force in 1966, and I found myself driving up to the radio station from Jefferson Road, which took about ten minutes. The station's driveway took visitors through acres of pasture, and there were cows around back! On my way there, I wondered, *Hey, is this a farm?*

I sat in the station general manager's office, across from his desk. He was a young guy of about twenty-five years old, with blond hair and blue eyes and a kind of cockiness about him, but he was very likable. His name was Bob Rowley. I later found out he was the son of the station owner, who had about seven newspapers in northeast Ohio.

"What kind of experience do you have?" he asked.

I took a deep breath and thought, *Well, here goes.* "I worked at WALG in Albany, Georgia, while I was stationed there in the air force," I said. "It was part-time; I worked Sunday mornings and weekends. I did everything from DJ to news."

I, of course, didn't tell him I was on the job only a few months and was fired. He'd have to really dig that out of me.

This job interview had come about as the result of pure chutzpah. My brother, Dennis, had a high-school girlfriend at the time I was leaving the air force to pursue my dream of becoming a broadcaster. His girlfriend's uncle, Bob Engle, was one of the leading radio newscasters in Cleveland, Ohio. Engle had spent many years on the number-one radio station in Cleveland, the station of my dreams, WHK. He now was the afternoon newscaster on the *new* number-one radio station in Cleveland, WIXY 1260. And he agreed to buy me lunch!

I had applied and been accepted to attend Columbia College in Chicago to pursue a bachelor's degree in broadcasting already. I was eager to get Engle's assessment of the school. We sat down for lunch at a Manner's Big Boy Restaurant on Vine Street in Willoughby, Ohio. I ordered a Big Boy hamburger and fries; he had coffee.

"College!" He laughed out loud. "No one in our business goes to college!"

The Big Boy, with its traditionally greasy tartar sauce, was creating a lump in my throat.

"No," he said, remembering, "one of the guys on our station *did* go to a college for a couple of months, but he dropped out. Everybody I've ever worked with who's successful in our business is qualified to work there because they have talent!"

"But how do they get jobs?" I asked.

"They just do. They walk into a small station like you did down in Georgia and say they want to work there. They get hired and work until they find a better job in a bigger market [a larger city] and move up. You don't quit your job until you find a better job! And you keep moving up until you land where you want to be.

"So," he said, matter-of-factly, as though it were simple, "just call around and get a job and continue your journey. You already have experience—it should be easy!"

That lunch was an eye-opener about the world of broadcasting. It exposed the man behind the curtain, so to speak. It was a business of talent, like show business, where people don't achieve success because they have a degree from a college, but because they sing, or act, or entertain so well that they have an audience. They are hired because they either already have an audience or can attract one. It's all about talent.

So that's what I did: I called around and got a job. I knew the big stations in Cleveland would not be interested in someone with a few months' experience playing Sam Cooke records between "The Tennessee Ernie Gospel Hour" in a small town in Georgia, so I started with stations outside of Cleveland.

Ashtabula's WREO was familiar to me. Our speech class had gone there during my senior year of high school to do a show. I had been the main announcer and had introduced the record *Dedicated to the One I Love* by the Shirelles. Before playing the record, I read the dedications my Wickliffe High School classmates had given to me. The WREO announcer who hosted the show, Mike Toby, seemed astonished that I read it so well and was a little cocky—he looked envious. As he began to cut me down a bit, he seemed awfully nervous saying, "Hey, kid, if you can do that without reading, you might have a career in this business."

I remembered this experience as an adult, and after I called a few stations, WREO was the one that sounded most interested. The station program director, Andy Holecko, said, "Can you come in for an audition?"

Holy cow! I thought, *They want me to come in?* Was it that easy? The audition had me reading scripts for news, opera, and classical songs. It was crazy, but it landed me in front of the young general manager.

"Well, Richard, we want to offer you a job," Bob Rowley said at the end of our meeting.

"Great!" I tried to contain myself.

He continued, "But there's one thing you have to agree to before we have a deal. You see"—he sat back in his chair—"this is a small station, and we are offering you the evening show on WREO, from seven to eleven at night. However, because we are small, you have to do more than that. Everyone here has additional duties, and you will have something else to do as well."

Now I was thinking he was going to ask me to clean the bathrooms or mow the giant front lawn. *At least they have a farm tractor*, I thought.

He looked me straight in the eyes.

Here it comes! I thought.

But he said, "You'll also have to do the weather on our TV station."

"TV station? You have a TV station here too?"

"Yes," he said, "but don't worry; no one watches except the old man."

His father, I thought.

"No problem," I exclaimed. "I'd love to!"

Did he check my references? No. Did he listen to a recording or air check of my performance on Johnny Reb Radio? No. Did he ask if I knew anything about weather? No. Did he ask if I was qualified to be a weathercaster on his TV station? No. Hey—Bob Engle had been right; I got the job because I had talent!

Oh, and one other thing: I couldn't use the names Richard or Rick—they already had those names on the staff—so my air name was Dick Michaels. (Michael is my middle name.) And my on-air nickname was Dickey Doo Michaels! I still get phone calls from people from back then, and the first thing they say is, "Dickey Doo, is that you?"

For my first full-time job in broadcasting, I was an evening disc jockey and TV weatherman. Guess how much money I was making.

Every week they cut me a check for seventy-eight dollars. That's $1.95 an hour, for a total of about $4,000 a year. The station was owned by the Rowley family, so we called our paychecks "Rowley coupons," a nickname some of my older readers will appreciate. (For some time, Raleigh cigarettes were popular, and the manufacturer gave away Raleigh coupons with every pack, which you could redeem for prizes.)

4

YOU'RE FIRED, AGAIN

...and during that time, I was fired and hired back in the same day!

I always wanted to leave WREO, but I actually worked there three times! I left the first time after four months to work forty-five miles up Interstate 90 at WWGO in Erie, Pennsylvania.

I worked at WREO for the second time before going to WMMS in Cleveland, which is the opposite direction from Erie on I-90, about fifty-three miles west.

And finally, after being fired by WMMS—an incredible story about managerial ineptitude that deserves its own chapter—I returned to WREO a third time. During this period, I was fired and hired back in the same day!

I've always had this problem in broadcasting. I have fun when I'm on the air; I just get a kick out of it. I forget all my problems and worries and take on a different personality. It's like David Letterman's character said in the movie *The Night Shift*: "It's the only time when I'm happy!" And besides, if you're not having fun, how can you survive on the wages they pay you?

One day, when I was on the air and having fun, I thought that when I played Bob Dylan's latest hit, "Lay Lady Lay," I would use the instrumental music leading up to his vocal by just slowly saying the title—simple, but effective. Back in those days, "Lay lady lay" *could have* suggested "Lay lady lay," but as you and I know, it actually meant just *innocently* "Lay lady lay." (I know you follow me!)

I started the record, the instrumental intro to Dylan's vocal began, and I said very slowly, "Here's Bob Dylan, with"—I spoke even more slowly now—"Lay…lady…lay…across…my…big…brass…bed." Then Dylan's voice came in, singing, "Lay lady lay…"

OK, so now I was proud of my creativity. However, when I looked up, the station manager was standing at the studio window, outrageously mad. The program director rushed in, yelling, "That's it; go down to the manager's office immediately! I'll take over here!"

When I reached the manager's office, he demanded, "I'll accept your immediate resignation!"

"Why do you want me to resign?"

"For what you just said on the radio."

"What? 'Lay lady lay'? That's the lyric of the song!"

"I don't care. You're done—unless you want to stay and be news director."

I walked out of his office as the new news director with an increase in pay! Don't ask me to explain this; I can't. I've thought about this event for years, and I think either broadcast management can't stand to see people happy or he just thought I was a better news anchor than disc jockey. I really don't know.

This very well could have been one of those miracles in my career where I was being drawn into the news business, which I had resisted. But, when I think back on it, somebody up there was telling me to get into news.

The second time the young manager wanted to fire me came, once again, as I was having fun on the air, now as a radio newsman.

I was reading the news on the air in the fast-paced, rock-and-roll style that was in vogue at the time. Each newscast was filled with taped sound bites of people in the news stories.

I had no more tapes to play in this newscast, but I thought I would have a little fun with the disc jockey who played the tapes for me. I put my arm high into the air as I was reading, in order to signal to him to get ready to play the next tape. The disc jockey, Jerry Allan, who looked and acted a lot like Albert Brooks, panicked. He looked around, could not find another tape, and started waving his arms in the air frantically to tell me there were no other tapes.

I started laughing uncontrollably, so much so that the newscast stopped, and I laughed out loud hysterically; he also laughed. The station manager came running over to the window with the meanest look on his face, and when we saw him, we laughed even harder. The mikes were still open; we were on the air laughing! And laughing at the boss is not good—*especially* when you're live on the air! The disc jockey played a record then, and yes, I was back in the manager's office.

"I have a good mind to make you pay for the sponsorship of that newscast!" he said. "We can't charge the sponsor for that; you made a fool out of them [I believe it was the East Ohio Gas Company] and me!"

I said, "How much would that be?"

He squirmed in his chair, his eyes shifting back and forth. "Six bucks!" he said.

Was he worried about losing six bucks, or was he ticked off that I was having such a good time and he wasn't?

Mostly, managers who are put in charge of creative minds are bottom-line-oriented businesspeople, technicians, and humorless drones, and sometimes they're mean! I guess they're just not having as much fun as the people who perform on air and are envious. But I have a discussion on the difference between talent and management coming up in a separate chapter. Stay tuned!

While working at WREO, I always wanted to leave, to move up—but come on, a stepping stone to Buffalo?

5

GO, GO, "GO RADIO!"

His pants were down to his skivvies, and then a shocker!

As I mentioned in chapter 4, I first left WREO after four months to head to WWGO, "Go Radio." It was a dump.

As it turned out, I was the only full-time radio announcer on the staff. I learned this after I started there. All the others were part-timers who came in for three- or four-hour shifts and were paid hourly.

One was a utility worker, one was a shoe salesman, one was a high-school student, and one was a high-school teacher who fancied himself the Frank Sinatra of Erie, Pennsylvania.

Even the station general manager was part-time! He was there only three days a week. His name was Larry Parratto, and he was a good-looking, smooth-talking sales guy who had talked me into taking the job because it was a step up and a good opportunity to move to Buffalo, which is not far from Erie. And besides, I got a raise, an extra twelve dollars; I was now making ninety bucks a week!

The station was located in the Commerce Building in downtown Erie, and I thought that was cool—working downtown, rather than in a cow pasture! However, it was equipped with stuff from the early forties:

olive-drab control boards and homemade equipment. The station was jerry-rigged with a combination of home-electronic and professional-broadcasting equipment.

When the chief engineer showed me around the station before my first air shift, he pointed out an extension cord that went from some equipment in the studio to a wall socket. "Whatever you do," he said, "don't trip on this cord where it might pull out of the socket."

I said, "Why? What will happen?"

"You'll knock the whole station off the air!" he exclaimed.

I said, "I'll never let that happen." But not long after that, I tripped on the cord and pulled it out of the socket. The whole studio went dark and silent. There was no juice into any of the equipment. This was not good for a pop radio station. I plugged it back in and kept on broadcasting. No one noticed!

Another thing I remember vividly was once, while on the air, I placed one hand on a tape-cartridge player and my other hand on a turntable. An electric current ran from my hand right through my body to the turntable! I was being electrocuted! I complained to the engineer.

He said, "Yeah, I know" and then ran off to his full-time job. To this very day, I never touch or hold an electronic device in each hand at the same time.

Why was it such a low-budget operation? The station was for sale. Parratto's job was to keep expenses low, make the bottom line look good, and get rid of the station.

However, in spite of the mess it was, I had the time of my life. And my entire life *was* the station. All the guys were my age or younger, and we palled around together, worked together, partied together, ate together, got in trouble together, brought our girlfriends to the station together, and did everything else together too. We were a close-knit group of guys having a ball learning broadcasting at such a young age.

But WWGO was a strange radio station. Case in point: One show we did every year was just bizarre and outrageous; it was a live, remote broadcast from the Erie Home Show. Back then, when you did a remote broadcast, you normally had a DJ and a record turntable or two, and the DJ played music and invited everyone to come on down.

Not at WWGO. Our broadcast consisted of blocks of time sold to the exhibitors of the home show to advertise their products. Some segments might have been five minutes, others ten minutes, and some fifteen minutes or more! Whatever the advertisers wanted to buy, our bright management would sell to them.

That year I was the first one on duty, in the morning, with a list of times and locations. I remember rushing into one booth to do fifteen minutes on an appliance dealer who sold washing machines and kitchen appliances. I had only a few seconds to get there. When I arrived, no one was there to be interviewed.

So I had to talk for fifteen minutes about these wonderful appliances; I was desperate! I wanted to talk to customers, but the show hadn't opened yet, so I would stop workers, movers—anyone who would talk to me. Finally, I started running out of people. I grabbed Ken Olowin, one of the DJs from the station who was there with me.

It went something like this:

"Hi, sir. What is your name?"

"Harvey," he said. "Harvey Smith. Drove down from Silver Creek, New York."

Already I was choking back laughter. "Well, Mr. Smith, what do you think of this wonderful washing machine?"

"I like it!"

"What do you use now?" I asked.

"Have the old lady go down to the creek and bang the clothes on the rocks!"

We both cried out in laughter; I put my hand over the mike and worked to regain control. I tried to continue.

Then he said, "If only I had electricity!" I just couldn't stop laughing after that.

I wonder if the people listening—if, in fact, there were any at all—actually thought that interview was legit.

Little did I know I was laying the groundwork for ad-libbing and speaking extemporaneously—developing, as they say, *talent*. These opportunities are lost today for youngsters coming into the business. And besides, the kids I see coming into the business today would never move away from home for ninety bucks a week! They want it all now.

We did so many outrageous things; it would require a separate book just to describe them all. And again, in my career, I was having fun, and it was the laughter that got me in trouble.

I remember one day I was doing the big noon newscast, which followed the big CBS noon newscast. As I read my news copy, I looked up, into the control room, and there was Ken Olowin standing on one of the giant turntables. As the turntable rotated, he began to pull down his pants! I started laughing—yes, the mike was open, and again I was laughing on the air. His pants were down to his skivvies, and then a shocker: the general manager, who happened to be in the station at the time, heard me laughing and came to see what was going on. Ken saw him peering through the window and tried to turn off the turntable. As he reached down for the switch, his pants got caught in the equipment, and the turntable chewed up his trousers. I was crying laughing. He would not, or perhaps could not, turn off my mike, so I disconnected the mike from its socket and ran out of the studio, laughing, right into the manager!

Mr. Parratto called a full staff meeting for later that day. "Listen, you guys, this laughing on the air, this horsing around, has got to stop." He looked above the top rim of his horn-rimmed glasses and said, "And you, Ken, standing on that turntable, with no pants..." Then he started laughing! We all laughed and promised it would never happen again.

It, of course, continued. The nighttime disc jockey, Rick Rutkowski, was one of the nicest guys you'd ever want to meet. He had changed his name to Rick Schaffer, and he sounded really mellow and smooth on the air. However, he did make a lot of little mistakes, so he called his show "Chaos and Confusion with Rick Shaffer." Or, perhaps, *we* called it "Chaos and Confusion," while *he* called it "Chaperone Schaffer." He, like me, was having too much fun!

One evening, when the day-side guys and I were leaving, we told him, "Now listen, Rick, when you're doing the eight o'clock news tonight, don't laugh; don't laugh, because we'll be listening!"

Later that night, after having dinner with all the guys, someone said, "Hey, it's coming up on eight o'clock!" We pulled the car over and listened. Rick started the eight o'clock news, and, you guessed it, he started to laugh, knowing we were listening!

One day, the station was flooded with calls because other offices in our building and in the buildings on the same block were getting our radio station on their telephones and PA systems; our broadcast was even bleeding through their radios when they were not listening to us.

It turned out that while Ken Olowin was on the air, he was also on the phone talking to his mother, who lived in another town many miles from Erie. We ran into the studio to find out what was happening. He had turned up the transmitter, the modulation equipment, and everything he could so his mother could hear him. "Can you hear me now, Mom?" he was yelling in the phone.

Another hilarious incident happened with Ron Seggi, a young and very talented DJ who was in high school at the time. He would come in after classes and do the afternoon show, and he was always sleepy because of his grueling schedule. Part of his show was an hour-and-a-half block of news from the CBS Radio Network, broken up into two or three shows. In between each show, there might be five or ten minutes to fill. His job was to do the station IDs and to read short newscasts and announcements during those breaks.

One day, he fell asleep on a couch outside the studio. He slept through not only the hour-and-a-half news block and the times he was supposed to be reading the news but through an extra half hour of dead air when it was over. Dead silence for a half hour! Afterward, he woke up, put on a record, and acted as if nothing had happened—and no one noticed.

Another member of our "gang" was Pat Rodgers, who actually didn't work at "GO"; he was the overnight DJ at a station across town, WWYN. I don't recall how we met, but we all hit it off, and he hung around with us.

One night, we were all out partying late, and Pat went in to do the all-night shift. At about three o'clock that morning, Pat put a record on, put his head down on the desk, and fell asleep. The record ran out, and the needle of the record player skipped to the label. All you could hear was the scratch of the needle, over and over and over again—for at least an hour. Listeners called the cops, who broke into the station, thinking Pat might have died. They found him slumped over on the desk. When one cop put his hand on Pat's shoulder, he startled Pat, who woke up to see a police officer staring down at him.

He had some "splainin'" to do to the boss the following morning.

Pat and I shared an apartment, and we always lost track of whose turn it was to do the dishes and other housework. When things got kind of seedy, our friends (female student nurses!) from Mercy Hurst College would come in and clean up, and we would have a party. It was a good time.

One day I got a call from a smooth-talking gentleman. "Rick, I just got out of the army, back from Vietnam, and I'm looking for a job in radio. Can I come over to the station and make an audition tape?" he asked.

"Sure!" I answered. I practically lived at the station, so I was always there.

"How about tonight?"

"Come on over!" I said.

About a half hour later, he arrived, and I walked him back to the production studio. "I'm Rick D'Amico."

"I'm Walt Shaw," he said, and we shook hands. I could tell he was a sincere, honest man. We had a long talk, and I liked him immediately.

I said, "Well, let's make a tape, and maybe we can get you in here at GO Radio!"

He paused for a long time and said, "I got to tell you something. I just came from another radio station in town, and they wouldn't even talk to me!"

"Why not?" I asked.

"Well," he said, "On the phone, they wanted to hire me because they liked my voice, but when they saw me, they seemed to turn cold."

"Why's that?" I asked.

He said, "I think it's because I'm black." I was outraged, thinking back to my time living in Georgia while in the air force.

We made a tape that I later played for the general manager. I talked Walt Shaw up, and he got the job. It turned out that Walter Lee Shaw was fantastic! When I left to go back to Ashtabula, he came with me. And then he went to Houston, LA, Detroit, and other major markets, and eventually he earned a nationally syndicated radio show. His air name was Walt Baby Love. Last I heard, Walt was the star of three nationally syndicated radio shows.

Pat Rodgers went on to be a big-time radio personality in San Antonio on WOAI, and then to be communications director for the Catholic diocese of San Antonio, Texas.

Ron went on to do a national radio show called "The Ron Seggi Show," which originated in Orlando.

Rick Schaffer distinguished himself by leaving broadcasting and becoming a nurse. No laughing on that job—well, maybe.

Ken Olowin owns and operates a successful advertising business in Erie, and his voice is still heard on Erie airwaves.

Another great talent I worked with briefly at GO Radio was Rick Scarry. Rick was also working at WWOW, "Wonderful W-Wow," in Conneaut, Ohio. The guy who owned W-Wow was a bit difficult, and if he had found out Rick was working at another station, he would have gone berserk. In order to keep his day job, Rick changed his name for our Erie audience to Lou Burdick.

Rick used to tell me stories about all the announcers he worked with in Armed Forces Radio, most of whom went on to become very successful in commercial radio and in acting in Hollywood when they got out of the service. Rick's dream was to someday become an actor. At the time of this writing, one of the most successful television dramas was *Mad Men*. Can you imagine my surprise when, watching an episode one evening, I saw Rick there on the show, playing Don and Betty Draper's neighbor? What a thrill!

WWGO was finally sold, and the transition was a terrible time. The station went without direction for a month or two, until the new owners got in place. It was so bad that I walked out and went home to Cleveland for two weeks! They called me every day and begged me to come back! I did, and stayed awhile.

In the meantime, WSEE-TV in Erie offered me a chance to come in and audition for a TV news-anchor opening. I did, and they offered me the job! I turned it down, because I wanted to stay in radio. Another one of those miracles from somebody up there urging me to get into television? Who knows?

The new owners of WWGO brought in this new program director; he was old—really old, like about seventy or eighty—and he wanted to coach me on how to "properly" speak on the air. His name was Skip Letcher. "When you say *W*, it's not *W*, it's *double youuuuu*," he'd say. And, "When you say 'temperature,' roll the *r* and say '*temperrrrrrrrrrature*'!" He sounded and looked like one of those announcers you see in a 1939 movie introducing a cello recital. This guy was a whack job! And, as you can imagine, this situation just wasn't perfect for me!

So here we go again. Who put this guy in charge? Management!

That was it; I'd had it, so I went back to Ashtabula.

6

VENUS VS. MARS: TALENT VS. MANAGEMENT

*...a cruel and shallow money trench; a long
plastic hallway where thieves and pimps run free
and good men die like dogs!*

Here are a few of my favorite stories about my own run-in with management. Because I desperately wanted to leave WREO in Ashtabula, Ohio, one day I had a luncheon appointment with the general manager and owner of radio station WPVL in Painesville, Ohio.

His name was Carl Lee. During lunch, he asked me about my duties at WREO.

"I gather the news from the wires and police radios and even visit the county sheriff's office daily as my beat, and I write the newscasts," I proudly said.

He looked me in the eyes as he puffed on his pipe. "Do you read it on the air?"

"Why, yes!" I said.

"Well," he said, "You couldn't do that on WPVL!"

"Why?" I asked.

Another puff on his pipe, the smell of which was totally disgusting while I was eating. He hit me with the bombshell: "Because your voice isn't good enough to be on the air!"

I don't remember what was said after that, because I was in shock. I think I went home and cried.

I've told this story on the air on the morning show in Phoenix, forty-something years later, after working on the air on radio and TV in some of the largest cities in the nation and for some of the largest companies, including CBS, FOX, and others.

But I wasn't good enough to be on the air in Painesville, Ohio! Says who? *Management!*

Here's another great story about management and talent. I was anchoring the noon and 5:00 p.m. newscasts on Channel 10 in Phoenix. One day I learned I was about to lose my job! I heard this from other staffers, not management.

I went to see the news director to ask him about this, and all he could tell me was "I can't answer that question." He suggested I talk to the general manager, who was new at the station.

The new GM, Ron Bergamo, told me he was hiring a new male anchor to replace the current evening anchor, Dave Patterson, and that Patterson, in turn, would take my position, and the GM really didn't know what my future would be. Oh, and by the way, when he told me about the new anchor he was hiring, he held up an eight-by-ten glossy of the guy—like he had just bought a shiny, new car.

Well, needless to say, this sent me and my family into a panic! I immediately began to make plans to find another job anywhere I could, even though uprooting my family was just horrible to me.

My work at the station had intensified as a reporter. I believe the news director, Dave Howell, and the assistant news director, Doug Drew, were trying to build my reputation as a reporter. They had sent me on reporting assignments like covering the 1992 riots in Los Angeles. I enjoyed the work.

After a few weeks, Bergamo called me into his office and told me the good news. "We did a research study and found the audience likes you and prefers you over Dave Patterson!"

Now, think about this. He wanted to replace Patterson, so he hired an anchor from Minnesota, when the audience preferred me over Patterson. What a waste of money, time, and talent.

Anyway, I was happy I could keep my job of anchoring the noon and 5:00 p.m. newscasts.

Does the general manager know talent? No. But *the audience* does. I never forgot that lesson. My allegiance was always to the audience, not management. The only way I've been able to keep my sanity and confidence over the years has been by listening to the comments made by regular people I've met in malls and supermarkets and on the streets, and on Facebook and Twitter, who tell me what and whom they like and what and whom they don't like.

The people of Phoenix have been very kind to me. Frankly, at the risk of bragging, there are times when I've simply been overwhelmed by people who have nothing but nice things to say about what I did on television. My trips to Costco alone often turn out to be stand-up gigs; people gather around, and I end up doing about twenty minutes of comedy!

Oh, by the way, not long after the fiasco of almost losing my job because of management's opinion, that general manager, Ron Bergamo, was fired by the station's new owners, and his new anchor from Minnesota left a few months later. And the female anchor he had also hired distinguished herself by becoming the fodder of a Phoenix broadcasting urban legend. Some twenty years later, I'm still asked if this really happened: One day, she was sitting at the anchor desk, about to read a thirty-second hourly update. The producer did not get her script to her in time. So she—brace yourself now, here it comes…here it comes—*hid under the anchor desk*! The news intro rolled on the air, and there was video of an empty anchor desk, while she crouched under the desk for thirty seconds because she didn't have a script! She had nothing to say. (She had an education—a master's degree in journalism from Northwestern University—but no talent.)

■ ■ ■

One of the most awarded and celebrated dramas in television history was AMC's *Mad Men*. It was about an advertising agency in the sixties. And my favorite line from the show is from the lead character, Don Draper, talking about management versus talent. Don says management "think[s] monkeys can do this. And they take all this monkey crap and just stick it in a briefcase, completely unaware that their success depends on something more than their shoeshine. *You* are the product. You feeling something. That's what sells. Not them. Not sex. They can't do what we do. And they hate us for it."

Because my career has been plagued by confrontations and disagreements with management, this hopefully will give you some insight as to why I've had such a hard time dealing with these strange people—why it just wasn't perfect for me.

"Talent" is the collective term used in broadcasting to refer to those who perform on the air. A DJ, reporter, or news anchor is talent. "Talent," in my opinion, is mostly a negative term from management's perspective. Management, generally speaking, does not like—or perhaps does not understand—talent.

Being in both positions in radio—talent while on the air, and management as a radio-program director and station manager—I've had to be on both sides of the table. There were times while sitting in conference rooms with CEOs, vice presidents, general managers, and others that I've listened to these people spew venom at how they felt about talent, and the same with broadcast performers against management.

I love Howard Stern's movie *Private Parts*, in which he refers to his boss as "Pig Vomit." I think "Pig Vomit" is being nice.

And my favorite quote of all time comes from Hunter S. Thompson: "The TV news business is a cruel and shallow money trench; a long, plastic hallway where thieves and pimps run free and good men die like dogs. There is also a negative side."

Here's my take on the difference between management and talent, mostly from my experience working at the local, station level.

I suspect that the two, management and talent, come from two different worlds. "Talent" are people who are performers. In order to be successful as a performer, you have to please people. The good performers really care about people and are keen observers of how people react to them, and they know pleasing people increases their popularity. And most of all, "talent" are people who are sensitive as to how they are accepted and approved by other people. Someone once said, "You're either here to serve people or you're not." The good talent are here to serve people. That's the only way they can become successful. And, by the way, talent most times are very insecure!

The lousy talent are those who make you ask the question "How did this person get that job?" The lousy talent are there only to serve themselves. I call them video masturbators or self-absorbed narcissists, and I've worked with plenty of them. How did they get the job? They were hired by management, who probably had the same character flaws! Read on.

"Management" are people who mostly care about numbers. They really don't think much about people. I once asked a management person what he thought of a new syndicated TV show. He answered, "Well, in Buffalo, it's getting a five rating with a seventeen in the demo, and in Chicago, it's getting a six with a twenty in the demo." He responded by giving me the show's ratings!

I said, "Yeah, but what do you think of the show: the chemistry of the cohosts, and how the show looks and feels?" He gave me a blank stare.

I've never seen or worked with a general manager, program director, or news director who got a promotion for doing good programming or good journalism. But, on the other hand, I have seen general managers, program directors, and news directors who have lost their jobs because the ratings have fallen or sales have gone down, and their profitability was lost.

So the two groups, "management" and "talent," just don't mix. That is why there have been so many missteps when it comes to management judging talent—for example, David Letterman being passed over by management for the *Tonight Show* for Jay Leno. Read the book and watch the feature film *The Night Shift*. The film and book are so true.

Then, Jay Leno left the *Tonight Show*, because NBC management decided Conan O'Brien would be better. Leno got a prime-time show, while O'Brien got Leno's show. O'Brien's ratings plummeted, and so did Leno's, so Leno went back to his old show, and O'Brien moved to cable.

Then Leno, at the peak of his career and the peak of his number-one ratings, was forced to step down to make way for a younger Jimmy Fallon. Was this the right move? Yes, but I can tell you this: the way NBC handled it was a shame.

On April 3, 2014, David Letterman announced to the world that he would retire in 2015. And in less than a week, the CEO and president of CBS, Leslie Moonves, announced he would be replaced by Stephen Colbert. Colbert had been the host of the *Colbert Report* on Comedy Central.

I was dumbfounded at this decision—why? Because Colbert at the time was not a real person; he was a character or a parody of a conservative reporter—an act. Moonves said Colbert would not use character but would become real and host the show as a real human being. If that's the case, how can Moonves (management, who, by the way, as I write this, makes upward of $60 million a year) justify hiring someone whom he's never seen perform in the genre he was hired for? Unbelievable! As Megan McDowell asked one morning on the *Don Imus Show*, "What if he's a jerk?"

I mentioned on our morning show in Phoenix that I didn't think Colbert even had a personality. And guess what? He played that clip on his show! It got a big laugh. And now I do think he's great on the air, but it's the manner in which he was selected that puzzles me.

Deborah Norville over Jane Pauley? Dan Rather over Walter Cronkite? And Dan Rather replaced by Katie Couric? During her tenure anchoring the *CBS Nightly News*, the ratings were the lowest since Douglas Edwards anchored the program in the sixties! NBC, by the way, seems to have a lousy track record when it comes to this; when Ann Curry was ousted from the *Today Show*, for example, it became another huge public-relations nightmare. NBC's *Today* show dropped to second place behind ABC.

The rumors were running rampant about David Gregory—that he was going to be replaced on *Meet the Press*. NBC denied them, saying something like, "David Gregory is in it for the long haul." Well, that long haul lasted about a month after the rumors started; then he was replaced. I don't know much about his talent, but I do know that, once again, NBC did an embarrassing job of replacing talent on a show.

How 'bout the Brian Williams fiasco? He basically was caught in a lie on national television. Not good for a network-television anchor. NBC management let him suffer for weeks without making a decision until they hired new management. In my opinion, NBC management should have put him right back on the evening news; had him make a big, sincere apology, saying something to the effect that he would work very hard to earn back America's trust; and then let the chips fall where they may. Instead, they banished him back to MSNBC where he had started.

And yet another example: Larry King was replaced by Piers Morgan, a citizen of the United Kingdom who denigrated our constitution on the air, made a complete fool of himself, and enjoyed the lowest ratings in that time slot for CNN. Morgan got fired! Oh really? Wouldn't you like to talk to the management person who hired him? What the hell was that person thinking?

Management doesn't seem to know or understand talent.

Also, there must be some type of resentment management has for talent; perhaps it's because they can't do what talent does.

Management doesn't know talent, and it's sad, but why? Because management supervises talent, and most members of management I've encountered over the years have no idea what talent's motivation is and how they think.

When talent become difficult to manage, it's not usually because they're bad people; the reality is that they're frequently insecure! And that insecurity comes when they get no support from management.

I've noticed in the brief history of Major League Baseball in Phoenix that team managers were let go because, as it was reported, they lost touch with their players and failed to motivate them. Major League Baseball players who were making millions of dollars a year still needed that touch—to be motivated, to be assured of their abilities. Many times, this is the difference between winning and losing.

Broadcast management is very much the same; they have very little in the way of motivational skills, and in most cases, the talent are just left alone to do their thing without any feedback. This causes resentment and friction.

One day, while I interviewed the great Tony Bennett—no doubt one of the most successful singers and musicians of all time—he told me of the moments before he went onstage at Carnegie Hall.

He said he was a nervous wreck. Orson Welles was standing backstage and noticed. Welles pulled Bennett aside and said, "I was over at Frank Sinatra's house not too long ago, and he always plays your records." Tony Bennett said he welled up with confidence and poise, went out onstage, and was just marvelous.

If Tony Bennett and million-dollar-salary Major League Baseball players need motivation, so does everyone else, no matter the job.

And I must add that my time at Fox Television in Phoenix, after a rough period in the beginning, was the best. The management team in the last years of my time there was just marvelous! There were times after our show ended when we were walking back into the newsroom that I thought for sure someone was going to hack my head off for some stupid thing I had said without thinking. I really admired our vice president of news, Doug Bannard; our executive producer, Mary Morse Vasquez; and our vice president and general manager, Mark Rodman, for being silent at those times and giving me the freedom to be bad, which, I believe, helped me to be good. It took a lot of patience and professionalism on their part to cope with me, and I will never forget how kind they were to me to allow me to thrive as a talent.

7

MAKING ROCK –AND– ROLL RADIO HISTORY! (WHO KNEW?)

"Rock and roll will never be successful on FM radio!"

I'm getting ahead of myself—now back to radio. The year was 1968. I was back at WREO in Ashtabula, Ohio, for a second time.

Ashtabula is about ninety miles east of Cleveland. Ashtabula had a population of about twenty-four thousand people; Cleveland had maybe a million, and it was a Top 10 market. To be on the air in Cleveland, the Rock-and-Roll City, was to die and go to heaven!

By this time, I had sent out hundreds, if not thousands, of tapes and résumés to radio stations around the country, trying to move up. Most responses, if there were any at all, were that they didn't like my voice; they typically said something about how it was too high and squeaky.

The rumor was out that WHK-FM (later to become WMMS-FM) in Cleveland was about to be one of the first FM stations east of the Mississippi to play rock-and-roll music. And I landed a job there! Wow!

Record-promotion guys used to come into WREO all the time. One of my duties at the time was serving as music director; I decided what records to play. One day, a very nice record-promotion man, Ernie Farrell, came in and played me some of the records he wanted us to air. I hit it off with him very well. I liked him and his songs, and I guess he liked me.

A few weeks later, he called to tell me of something new happening in Cleveland. WHK-FM was going to split from WHK-AM, discontinue playing elevator music on an automation machine, and instead become its own rock-and-roll station. And they needed disc jockeys. He said he'd put in a good word for me with the new program director, Pat McCoy, and told me to give McCoy a call in a few days. I did, and he called me in for an interview and lunch.

I got the job. Interesting: I was nice to the record-promotion man, who put in a good word for me to the new boss, who hired me based on personal knowledge from a friend. See how that works? This is a recurring theme in my career.

The station was kind of a mess. It was brand-new and was operating out of one of WHK's tiny studios.

My goal for my entire career had been to work at WHK. This was the station I had listened to as a kid in high school. This was the station that had the world's most amazing disc jockeys when I was growing up, including Mad Daddy Pete Myers and Johnny Holliday, my all-time radio idol. I wanted to be just like Holliday. I thought if I could just make it to Cleveland and WHK, that would be the end, the zenith, the best I could do.

I would walk through the hallways thinking, *Wow, Johnny Holliday walked this very same hallway! This is the studio where he worked; he called it his "Glass Cage."*

But this was not *the* WHK. This was WHK-FM, soon to become WMMS-FM, and no one really knew what he or she was doing. What can you expect? It was all new. The station was going to be free-form rock; blues; and what we called "underground radio" or AOR, album-oriented rock.

The disc jockeys McCoy hired were antiestablishment, counterculture-type personalities, but I have to tell you, they were amazing!

I remember Victor Boch. He was kind of glassy-eyed, spoke softly, and had weird hair, but he was very engaging on the air.

And then there was Doc Nemo—a gregarious, outrageous guy who was just crazy.

And one of the most talented guys I have ever met was Billy Bass. Bass was fun to listen to just in a one-on-one, in-person conversation—so you can imagine how entertaining he was on radio.

Much has been written about WMMS. It became historical, a legend of rock-and-roll radio stations in the United States. The book and television documentary *Radio Daze: Stories from the Front in Cleveland's FM Air Wars*, written by Mike Olszewski, do an excellent job of chronicling WMMS's history.

But in all fairness, although we were the pioneers who got it started, we kind of screwed it up! McCoy had never been a program director before, but, honestly, there were not too many people in the country who had experience with this kind of radio anyway.

And the weird, counterculture radio personalities had these strange experiences; they all wore the hippie clothes of the era (bell-bottoms and odd shirts) and had long hair, beads, and funny-smelling cigarettes. All except one—one who came to work every day in a suit and tie, had short hair, and was kind of straitlaced. That was me! I really didn't fit in.

McCoy filled the studio with hundreds of albums, put them in a big shelving unit in the back of the studio, and said, "There you go, guys; play this stuff." And that was basically it.

I had never been exposed to anything like this before. I was a fast-talking, Top 40 radio personality, and I was used to tight playlists, with every record chosen because it was currently a hit, was going to be a hit, or had been a big hit (oldie).

There were no jingles singing how great the station was, only a slogan voiced by Tim Taylor, who proclaimed, "You're listening to WHK-FM...a new groove!" Taylor, WHK-AM's news director, went on to distinguish himself as a prime-time news anchor on WJW-TV, a Fox station in Cleveland.

Oh, and there were no commercials either. No one knew who would listen; our salespeople were trying to figure out who would buy advertising!

And to make things even worse, WHK-AM and WHK-FM were union stations, which meant DJs could not operate the control board, which mixes the sound and sends it to the transmitter. We placed the albums on the turntables, cued up the cuts, opened our mikes, and hoped the engineer on the other side of the studio window opened up the sound so you could hear the music.

It was crazy. They usually sent the oldest or worst engineers to run the board on my show. I was always stuck with a guy named Fred, an older gentleman who didn't have a clue as to what was happening. He would just get up and wander off. One time, I opened my mike and introduced the song, and there was no sound. And where was Fred? He had wandered off again! So I yelled, on the air, *"Fred! Fred!* Come back and put up the sound...*Fred! Fred!* Where are you, Fred?" And Fred started to get fan mail!

I came on at 10:00 a.m. following the morning show with Victor Boch. That was interesting. One morning, while I was walking by the engineer on my way to the studio, he cried out, "You better get in there; I think he's dead!"

I walked in, and where was Victor? The lights were off, and a candle was burning, and there was Victor, lying flat on his back on the floor with his eyes closed. I thought he had died.

"Victor, are you all right? Victor, Victor!"

"Oh, hi, Rick!" he said softly. I took over, and he went home.

One evening, I decided to show my family the studios. We walked by the window, and there was Billy Bass, on the air, with an arm around the most beautiful girl, holding a bottle of wine in his other hand!

The management called a meeting one day in the general manager's office. We were all there, and so were the suits, general manager, AM program director, chief engineer, marketing director, FM program director, sales manager, and maybe even some corporate people.

Before the meeting got underway, as we all exchanged pleasantries, someone brought up a current story in the news about the pollution in Lake Erie. And Doc Nemo broke the ice by proclaiming, "Lake Erie *is* dirty! Do you know why?"

"No, why?" the Ivy League–graduate, suited general manager inquired, expecting an intellectual response.

"Because fish fuck in it!"

No one in management laughed, but I was choking. They were all buttoned-down, corporate people who really didn't get us.

Sometimes, the general manager, Dick Jantzen, would rush into the studio and yell, "I smell something coming out of the air-conditioning vents. Are you guys smoking pot in here?"

"No, Boss, it's incense," Nemo would answer.

I don't believe Jantzen would have known the difference anyway!

Pat McCoy, the program director, reminded me of Lou Grant from the *Mary Tyler Moore Show*. Yes, he had to be gruff to deal with the weird talent, but he was a nice guy. When he got frustrated, he would call Linda, the receptionist, into his office, wrap his arms and legs around her, and act like he was humping her, like they were having sex. She would scream, and we all thought it was fun. Apparently, his wife didn't think so; she divorced him, and Pat married the receptionist!

Being a radio broadcaster, I kind of could tell the station was doomed. The big indication? There were no advertisers to speak of. No commercials! And if there were, they were for small businesses, such as Joe and Eddie's Used Cars.

My wife needed a car, so I thought, *Why not go to one of our sponsors?* One of our ad salespeople took me to Joe and Eddie's on the west side of Cleveland. Joe or Eddie, I'm not sure which, appeared to me to be a little shaky. I told him I needed a car for my wife.

You know what he said? Sitting in the glass-enclosed office, looking down on the entire lot of maybe seventy-five used cars, he said, "You don't want anything on this lot!"

"What?" I asked.

"You don't want anything on this lot. I'll call you in a couple of days; I'll have a good car for you."

A few days later, he called. "I got a car for you; stop by the lot, and I'll give you the keys. You have to go and pick it up. It's parked outside some guy's house." He wanted me to repossess the car!

I told him, "I can't do that; I might get shot!" So he got it and had it ready for me at the dealership. And I bought it. It was a Volkswagen bug, and while my pregnant wife was driving it on the freeway in the middle of a snowstorm, the accelerator fell off!

The station named a new general manager, Ken Gaines. Ken used the name of Ken Scott on the air, and he was a fast-talking, Top 40 DJ who loved AM radio and hated FM—and hated us! This was yet another management change signaling doom for my job.

We had no ratings still, so McCoy got a bright idea to have a concert and invite potential advertisers so they could see who our audience was— big mistake! The coup d'état came the night of the big concert.

Next to WHK's studios was a giant ballroom used in the early days of radio for big-band concerts and dances. We renamed it the Grande Ballroom East and booked acts whose music was featured on our station. It was a free concert, and thousands showed up. The place was packed, and the crowd overflowed into the street. The problem was that they appeared to be hippies—counterculture kids smoking dope and screaming to the music, or so it seemed. It was a mini Woodstock! The management was appalled, the potential advertisers got scared, and the station was doomed.

The buttoned-down corporate people of WHK thought they could never sell advertising based on that audience.

But a really happy note about my time at WMMS: WHK-AM's program director's secretary liked me. Her name was Sunny Bombay; that's right—Sunny Bombay. I know it's a strange name, but she was not a stripper. Honest! And she liked me a lot. I mean, a lot!

One day when I was leaving the station, I failed to say good-bye to her. I drove home to Wickliffe, about thirty miles from our downtown studio. I was living with my mother at the time, but no one was home; I walked upstairs and crashed on my bed. A few moments later, I felt someone sit on the side of my bed.

"Hi, Mom," I said.

"Hi." But it was not my mom's voice.

I turned around, and there was Sunny Bombay, sitting on the side of my bed!

"Oh my God! Get out of here before my mom comes home!" I exclaimed.

Because I didn't stop by her office to say good-bye, she followed me home, about thirty miles! She walked right in the house, right upstairs to my bedroom, and joined me on my bed. After this, we both went downstairs, and she left. (I'm not kidding!) I guess she liked me a lot, which helped me to fulfill my all-time dream.

One day, she told me WHK-AM needed a DJ and that, being the secretary to the boss of the AM, she'd put in a good word for me. I got the job. So in addition to working WMMS-FM full time, I was also doing the overnight shift on WHK-AM on weekends.

This was a huge thrill. There I was in the same studio of the all-time great Cleveland DJs. WHK-AM had long since abandoned its Top 40 format, losing to Cleveland powerhouses WIXY-1260 and WKYC and to the Detroit/Windsor fifty-thousand-watt station CKLW. It had adopted a new format called "the Good Life," which involved Frank Sinatra, Tony Bennett, Jack Jones, Eydie Gormé, and songs we today call "the great American songbook." I loved it.

Working the overnight shift in a Top 10 market was challenging. One, you had to stay awake. Two, you had to deal with all the nuts who called the station in the middle of the night because they were lonely. Many of them were women who wanted to meet DJs at the back door of the station. I had learned my lesson the hard way in Ashtabula: when they showed up, they never matched the sound of their voice.

But I thought I was in heaven; not more than three years after I started my career, I had reached my goal in radio, that of working at my dream station.

However, my time in Cleveland was coming to an end. The management of WMMS-FM changed formats to Top 40, which didn't last long. About a year after we went on the air, it all came crashing down.

One day, I was on the air on WMMS, and Clem, a nice engineer, was working on the old automation equipment outside the studio. It was the machine the station had used to play background elevator music before we started our radical, underground-rock format.

"What are you doing, Clem?" I asked.

"Didn't they tell you?"

"Tell me what?"

"They decided to go back to elevator music and let all you guys go," he said sadly.

That's how you find out you're fired in broadcasting—not by management, but by friends or people you work with. Not long after that, we were all let go, just as Clem had said.

I remember the meeting. Ken Gaines, the general manager, sat at his desk. Behind him were all the suits, the managers of the entire operation. He was surrounded like you might see when the president of the United States makes an announcement, with all his people there to support him. And here comes the announcement from Gaines: "Rock and roll will never be successful on FM radio!" Can you believe that? *Rock and roll will never be successful on FM radio!* "You're all going to be let go," he said. "WMMS is going back to beautiful music." He meant elevator music. This just wasn't perfect for me!

Ken Gaines: clearly a man with real insight into the future. Whatever happened to him?

I went back to Ashtabula for a few months. In that time, WMMS became an automated station, playing background music, then pop music, and later, back to album rock under the guidance of some of the most brilliant programmers. It eventually became one of the most popular and well-known rock stations in American radio history.

I guess we were just a little too much, too early; we were, as they say, before our time.

8

HAVING FUN, AND THE MOST IMPORTANT PERSON IN MY LIFE

She had long—really long—blond hair, a gorgeous smile, and the most beautiful blue eyes I had ever seen.

After my time at WMMS, WREO in Ashtabula was eager to take me back for a third time. Really and truly, they were too nice! I stayed there a few months before moving on to Battle Creek, Michigan. (I always wanted to leave the cow pasture!)

Before signing off on WREO, I have to tell you some of the bizarre highlights of the three times I worked there and how I met the most important person in my life.

This is why I love radio people.

One of the rites of passage into the world of broadcasting was the old cliché of lighting the news copy on fire. You hear a lot of stories about that; some probably never really happened, but it actually happened to me.

Brad Elliott was the evening jock when I started at WREO just out of the air force. Elliott was from New York City and claimed to have worked with the nationally famous Cousin Brucie—Bruce Morrow, the very popular evening-radio personality on WABC in New York City. As

I write this, Morrow is still on the air on SiriusXM radio. Elliott told me stories of working with Morrow and the other WABC DJs.

I trusted him as a friend, so why I would suspect him of doing anything to sabotage my work? Think again!

One evening, I was doing an evening newscast on Elliott's shift, and while I was reading the news copy, ripped off the AP or UPI wire, he walked in, lit the script on fire with his Zippo, and started laughing out loud.

I jumped out of my chair, started screaming, and ran from the studio, announcing the required WREO News sign-off: "That's what's happening. I'm Dick Michaels, Ninety-Seven News!"

Elliott stood there stunned, because he was standing in the newsroom—nothing was on the air—not knowing what to do but panic. He froze. I grabbed a fire extinguisher, ran back in, and blasted the fire out. The mike was still open; the audience could hear the whole thing!

Today, of course, there is no news copy, no paper at all; everything is on a computer screen. How do you sabotage that?

Other guys I worked with at WREO were just amazing. Bob Belz, the morning personality, had a show called *Belz and Eggs*. He was one of the funniest guys in the business. He used a joke service for DJs called "Ideas Ink." We shared it with another service called "Contemporary Comedy." Those gag lines still popped up in my mind as I did the morning show on KSAZ-TV in Phoenix forty-four years later: "Ron Hoon has the news for you; he's the only guy in TV who can eat a banana sideways!"

Bob had a Polish-sausage stand at Geneva-on-the-Lake, Ohio, and he would end his show by saying, "Have yourself a ginger peachy day…stay tuned for big Dick Michaels, and see you at the Wang Stand!" Oh my God, can you say that on the radio?

Other wonderful people I worked with were Bob Cannon, who took me under his wing when I started at the station and introduced me to the real ways of radio; Jerry Allen, who I mentioned earlier, an Albert Brooks look-alike; Phil Knight, who the station hired because he had a good voice calling the drag races at Thompson Drag Raceway; Barely Human Berry Newman, who helped me move on to a great little station in Battle Creek,

Michigan; and Bob LaSalle, "your record-spinning pal," who came to us right out of the army from Vietnam, cane and all, and was an outstanding newscaster.

And then there was the hippie, Little Bobby. One day, he came running into the studio, all out of breath, scared as hell.

"Are you OK?" I asked.

"No, I was sitting in my apartment when there was a rapping on my door. Someone shouted, 'FBI!' I ran out the back door and took off!"

"What the hell does the FBI want with you?"

"I'm a draft dodger!" he exclaimed.

There were days when he told me he had relapses of being high while driving to work; the highway would start rolling up and down like he was on a roller coaster. He would say, "I didn't think I was going to make it to work!"

And, of course, my favorite coworker there was Lou Massey. No one could match Lou for being one of the most fun-loving and full-of-life people on the air or off. Lou was probably the only on-air talent I know who actually had more fun than I did while on the air. He was extremely talented and very successful, because he loved people and always talked about the people he met out in public: "Got to say hello to the guys at Treazi's Meat Market; got a good deal on some Sicilian sausage!" (Lou's real last name is Massiello!)

Lou and I shared a cottage on the shores of Lake Erie at Geneva-on-the-Lake, Ohio. We would throw these big parties, which we called steak and spags. We'd charcoal steaks, make a big pot of spaghetti, and invite everyone over, and we'd have a ball. We'd eat and drink wine all night long.

One morning, after such a night with what seemed like hundreds of guests, we, of course, were sleeping in. A neighbor decided to mow his lawn on a riding mower, which woke us both up, and Lou was incensed. He grabbed his BB gun and, through the back door, opened fire! We rolled on the floor laughing. No one in our neighborhood mowed their lawn in the early morning after that. Lou and I still keep in touch; he visits Phoenix every now and then, and we have lunch at my favorite Italian restaurant, Aiello's. When my mother died in July 2012, Lou came to the funeral. He's a great guy.

The Supermen—that's what they called the disc jockeys at WREO—were the MCs at the Ashtabula County Fair one year. I waited backstage to introduce the big act, Bobby Vinton, a Polish singer out of Canonsburg, Pennsylvania.

By this time, Vinton was an outstanding success, with a bunch of Top 40 hits; some, such as "Roses are Red," had been popular while I was in high school, and others caught the public's attention while I was in the air force.

So there I was backstage, and there was Vinton, ready for me to introduce him, and he was holding a bottle of wine. I said, "Hi, Bobby. I'm Dick Michaels. I'm going to introduce you tonight."

"Hi, Dick, you want a swig?" he asked.

"Sure!" I grabbed the bottle, took a drink, and gave it back to him. He took another drink, and I went out onstage and said, "Ladies and gentlemen, it's time now to bring out the main event of the evening. I was just backstage talking with him, and he is eager to come out here and meet you and sing his biggest hits." The crowd was screaming. "Ladies and gentlemen…Bobby Vinton!"

Vinton came out and took the crowd by storm, and I went home thinking, *He's one of the biggest entertainers of the time, and he was actually nervous! He had to drink a little wine to calm him down.* I realized, *Wow! Nervous is good.*

The record companies loved us. We played new hits first, and the promotion men would use this to get airplay on the bigger stations in Cleveland. In turn, they paid us back by giving us special treatment when big stars came to town.

Steve Popovich, a legendary Cleveland, Ohio, record executive, invited us to see Gary Puckett and the Union Gap perform at a nightclub in downtown Cleveland. At the time, Puckett had some huge hits, including "Woman, Do You Have Cheating on Your Mind?" and "Young Girl."

I sat at a table watching him and his group perform. On my right was a popular WKYC Radio Cleveland DJ, Chuck Dann. On my left was a stranger, an older gentleman who sang along with the group and was

IT JUST WASN'T PERFECT FOR ME   47

totally immersed in their performance. He would, from time to time, look at me and softly comment on the songs, how they were written, and how Puckett sang them.

Chuck Dann leaned over to me and whispered in my ear, "Do you know who that is sitting next to you?"

I had no idea. "Who?"

"It's Buck Ram!"

Buck Ram was a legendary songwriter and arranger who had written most of the Platters' big hits, and he was also Puckett's manager. It's been said that the history of rock and roll could not have been written without Buck Ram. He wrote and produced for such performers as the Coasters, the Drifters, Tina Turner, Duke Ellington, Glen Miller, Ella Fitzgerald, and many others. For the Platters, he wrote "Only You," "The Great Pretender," "Magic Touch," and "Twilight Time"—songs that were a big part of my life when I was a teen. And here he was talking to me! I was having a drink and socializing with Buck Ram! What a memorable evening!

Another night I will never forget was when Ernie Farrell, the record-promotion man who had helped me get the job at WMMS, invited us to a party to welcome Dionne Warwick to Cleveland. She was a huge recording star with such hits as "Do You Know the Way to San Jose." *Billboard Magazine* credits her as being second only to Aretha Franklin as the most charted female vocalist, with fifty-six singles making the Billboard Hot 100 between 1962 and 1998.

The party was in a nightclub on Cleveland's lakefront. We all stood around schmoozing one another, waiting for Warwick to appear. She then made her grand entrance; DJs, radio-station-management people, and record executives from all over northeastern Ohio and the West Coast were watching as she walked right up to me first, extended her hand, and said, "Hi, Dick, I'm Dionne Warwick!" I almost fainted.

WREO had a couple of strange weekday programs that most of the disc jockeys hated but that I thought were fun: *Swap Shop* and *Polka Time!*

Swap Shop was a one-hour show in which people would call in live on the air and either sell or ask to buy things. For example, callers might say,

"I need to buy a carburetor for a 1959 Ford," or, "I'm looking to buy a bassinet for a newborn." I would sometimes host this show, and at times, the calls were questionable.

One day a man called in and said, "I have for sale a 1966 Henway, which I will sell for a hundred dollars or best offer."

I paused and then asked, "What's a Henway?"

And the voice on the other end said, "Oh, about two and half pounds!"

I looked over to one of the production studios, and there were Bob Belz and Lou Massey on the phone, laughing like crazy. It was them putting me on, live on the air!

Andy Holecko, the program director, hosted a daily show called *Polka Time!* One day he said, "Dick, I'm going to be off next week, and I want you to do my show."

I, of course, said yes. So there I was, doing a polka show. I changed my name from Dicky Doo Michaels to Dicky Doosky for the show. "Hi, everybody, it's Dicky Doosky on *Polka Time!* Here's Frankie Yankovic, who once dated my aunt Rose, with 'The Beer Barrel Polka.'"

Young adults starting out in the business today often ask how I was able to do a live three- to five-hour morning show on TV, be glib, speak extemporaneously, and go with the flow. It was this experience working at small stations such as WREO in Ashtabula, Ohio, and WWGO in Erie, Pennsylvania, that was so invaluable. Today, it seems that only a handful of companies own all the radio stations in the country, and many are automating their stations. With young workers these days wanting to start out on top, this opportunity for young talent to make mistakes and hone their skills is lost, and it's a shame.

WREO was also a major station of the Cleveland Indians Baseball Network. With its powerful FM signal, the station covered all of northeastern Ohio and northwestern Pennsylvania. Other radio stations, such as WWYN in Erie, Pennsylvania, would pick up the games off our FM and rebroadcast them to their audience.

Remember WWYN? That's where my friend Pat Rodgers worked. During the games, when I was operating the control board, inserting commercials and station breaks, I usually got really bored. Baseball on radio can be truly boring. It has a lot of downtime, with nothing happening and plenty of crowd noise.

So I would try to make things interesting. I would gather sound effects and insert them in the game—you know, to add color! "It's the windup, and the pitch, and..." then you would hear an explosion. "It's a line drive to center field." Sometimes, I would throw in a "boing" just for variety.

During downtimes, when the announcers paused, you would just hear the sound of the crowd in the stadium, and I thought that needed a little spice, so I would insert cows mooing and, every now and then, a rooster crowing.

And my favorite thing to do during pauses in the game was to open my mike, turn it down low, and make an announcement as though I were the stadium PA announcer. "Pat Rodgers, please report to the information desk; we found your bowling shoes!"

On one such occasion, the station hotline rang, and I answered. It was Pat Rodgers, calling from Erie, Pennsylvania. "What the hell are you doing?" he asked. He was laughing like crazy.

What do you suppose all the Cleveland Indians fans were thinking, all over northeastern Ohio and northwestern Pennsylvania? They probably thought that was all real!

Another show WREO ran was the syndicated *Earl Nightingale: A Changing World*, which came on after the noon news. I would play it before going back into music. I would sit there as a captive audience and listen to Nightingale's message of positive thinking, of achieving success in business and in one's personal life. He also preached his core message, "You become what you think about," or "You are the sum product of your thoughts!" This message has stayed with me to this very day, and it is one of the prime reasons I have achieved any success at all. I am deeply indebted to Earl Nightingale and to WREO for having the insight to run such a wonderful program. Another one of those miracles in my life?

■ ■ ■

But above and beyond all the fun and the people I met, there was one person who changed my life forever.

It was my second stint at WREO, after I came back from WWGO in Erie, Pennsylvania. On my first day back, I was walking with Bob Belz to the studios when the door opened and hit me right in the face. On the other side of the door was the most beautiful girl I had ever seen in my life.

She had long—really long—blond hair, a beautiful smile, and the most amazing blue eyes I had ever seen.

"Well, you just ran into 'the flower child,'" Belz exclaimed.

"Hi," I said.

She nodded; said, "Hi"; and kept walking. I was stunned. Her name was Ruth Roboski. She was about five years younger than me, and she was a picture of beauty and grace. I fell in love with her that moment.

The DJs called her "the flower child," or "Flo" for short. She took calls for the jocks and did some on-air announcing. After a newscast, you would hear a ballsy announcer say, "More music now," and her voice on tape screaming, "Dickey Doo Michaels!" and then a jingle singing, "Woopie."

She pranced through the station, with short skirts that showed her long legs, all beautiful long, blond hair and soft blue eyes, and all the guys would swoon. And I thought, *She's the type of girl who marries a doctor or a lawyer; she would never go for a simple, blue-collar guy like me.* I thought I would never have a chance with her.

She was going with Dave Allen, the midday DJ, at the time. I was the music director, a position that is second in command to the program director. The midday DJ's shift was 10:00 a.m. to 2:00 p.m., so during her lunch break, she would sit in the studio with Allen while he was on the air. One day, I got up some courage, walked into the studio, and said, "Hey, Flo, the rules are you're not supposed to be in here while the jock is on the air." So she went down to the lunchroom. And guess who decided to go to the lunchroom and sit next to her. Yeah, me! But I never had enough courage to ask her out; I was just too shy.

Pat Cooper (Pasquale Caputo), an Italian comedian who was famous for his recording of "The Italian Wedding," was a big act in Las Vegas and a frequent guest on national TV talk shows. He also appeared in movies; the most recent was *Analyze This*, with Robert De Niro. Cooper had relatives in Ashtabula who owned a restaurant, and he would appear on our shows on WREO. Afterward, he would invite us to lunch at his restaurant.

One day, Cooper was playing at a nightclub in Cleveland, and he invited us all to come and see his show. All the guys were bringing their wives or girlfriends. I wanted to take Ruth, but I was too shy to ask her, so Bob Belz asked her for me. She said yes. Who knows if she really wanted to see Cooper or have a date with me?

We went and had a wonderful time. Cooper invited us to his dressing room before and after the show, and we all went out to dinner afterward. That was the beginning of a yearlong courtship.

Ruth's father didn't approve of me. After a time, I got fed up with the tension and decided to go move her out of her house while her parents were gone. My little sports car was loaded with all her clothes and what seemed like thousands of stuffed animals.

Imagine the look on my mother's face when I walked into her house in Wickliffe, Ohio, with Ruth and all her belongings and proclaimed, "Ruth and I are moving in until we find an apartment!"

We got married on May 2, 1969. We ran away to Monroe, Michigan, as Ruth was too young to get married in Ohio, and a happy judge pronounced us man and wife.

My mother was incensed. "Oh my God, not being married in a Catholic church means you're not married at all!" Not long after that, we exchanged vows again in Our Lady of Mount Carmel Catholic Church in Wickliffe, Ohio.

Ruth has been everything a man could ever want in a wife and by far the best thing that's ever happened to me. She is everything I ever wanted or could hope for.

As I look back on all the adventures we've been on, like picking up and moving across the country, and even moving *out* of the country for a broadcasting job, I see how she stood with me and supported me, and how she still to this day encourages me. Many wives of radio and TV people just don't put up with the instability, but Ruth is always there as a rock and a real compass. She brings me down to earth and reminds me of who we really are—a father and mother earning a living to give our children the best life we can.

I love her very much. And I still see the beautiful long blond hair and soft blue eyes; when she smiles, she makes me very happy. I'm still, to this day, after forty-seven years of marriage, amazed she would have anything to do with me!

9

THE CEREAL CAPITAL OF THE WORLD AND KEENER RADIO

Using every four-letter word he could think of, including the f-word, he screamed into the phone, and yes, that was going over the air along with **Paul Harvey News and Comment.**

It was a beautiful summer day in Michigan. Ruth and I made a left turn off I-69, heading west on I-94. It was like driving through a forest: huge, tall trees everywhere, so green and full, and a blue sky with white, fair-weather clouds looking down on us. If it weren't for the billboards along the freeway, you would think nothing was out here, just miles and miles of trees—how beautiful.

Then came I-194 and a lump in my throat. We made the turn north. And shortly, there were those two tall skyscrapers emerging above the trees, signaling a major metropolis was just over the horizon. However, it wasn't a major city at all; it was a city of about fifty thousand people, and it was known worldwide as the Cereal Capital of the world—Battle Creek, Michigan.

The date was August 6, 2009. Ruth and I drove in from Cleveland, Ohio, where we had celebrated my mother's ninety-sixth birthday. The very next day, August 7, would be the Keener 14 Radio Reunion.

It had been at least twenty-nine years since we'd lived in Battle Creek, and I was very emotional. It's hard for me to describe why. Ruth and I lived there just after our first daughter was born, from 1970 to 1980, with one brief interruption, which was an adventure I'll tell you about later.

Those ten years were the most rewarding professionally and personally for us. We had friends there whom we love to this very day. The memories of running one of the most storied and coolest radio stations in the country will remain with me forever. This little one-thousand-watt radio station in one of the smallest towns in America had a reunion, and former employees came from all over the country to reminisce and renew. It was one of the best times of my life.

Today, after I've lived in a burgeoning metropolis of over four million people for more than thirty years, Battle Creek, Michigan, is for me an almost perfect city.

The Kellogg Company has made the downtown just beautiful, in my view. And the forested lakes and neighborhoods are just gorgeous. It's a small town where everyone seems to know everyone. Many of the towns-people meet every morning in one coffee shop to share stories before starting their day, and yet the city still has a cosmopolitan feel. Not far from the city, there are rolling hills, beautiful farms, and just wonderful people.

My thoughts went back to 1970. I was on my third and last gig at WREO in Ashtabula, Ohio; our first child had just been born on April 15; and I asked the management for a raise. Instead of a raise, they offered me a part-time job selling background music to department stores. Oh, brother, that was fun! I would walk into stores in the Greater Cleveland far-east side and tell them I was from "Music Air" of Ashtabula. They would say, "We have 'Muzak'" and laugh me out of the store. No one wanted "Music Air."

I had sent tapes and résumés out to radio stations all over the country. When I got an offer to go to KORL in Honolulu, Hawaii, it sounded great, but it paid about a hundred bucks a week. "Gee, isn't it expensive to live in Hawaii?" I asked the program director on the phone.

"Yeah, but don't you have a relative here you can live with?" he asked.

This was at about the same time the know-it-all station manager/owner at WPVL in Painesville, Ohio, told me my voice wasn't good enough to be on the air there.

I had rejection letters from all over the country saying, "Your voice is too high and squeaky," and I was considering quitting broadcasting altogether and going to work with my brother-in-law. Tomas Tarantino, known as Tomaz to all of us who love him, is perhaps the nicest man I've ever known, and I'm lucky to have him in my family. He married my sister, Diane, and he was—and is—a major influence on all our family. I loved him and respected him then as I do today.

He was the union steward for the teamsters' truck drivers at the *Cleveland Plain Dealer* newspaper. He told me a hundred times, "Richey, I got a job for you. You take the papers off the conveyer belt and load them on the truck—fifty thousand a year! And after a while, you get your own truck and a raise."

I was this close to taking that job and giving up on my dream.

Thank God for afternoon WREO Ashtabula DJ Barely Human Berry Newman. He had just landed a job at Keener Radio, and he was all excited. Keener was known among most Top 40 DJs in the country as a hot and great station to be on; however, the best-known Keener station was Keener 13 in Detroit—not Keener 14 in Battle Creek!

"Keener, wow!" I said to Barry as he showed me the letterhead describing his job offer. "*The* Keener?"

"Well, it's not Keener in the Motor City; it's Keener in the Cereal City!"

Keener 14 WKFR was a sister station to the big Keener in Detroit. Both were owned by the same owner and were programmed similarly. The station had the same jingles and sounded almost the same. But there was one big difference: Detroit was WKNR, and Battle Creek was WKFR. (I should note here that later, when Detroit's WKNR changed call letters, Battle Creek's WKFR changed its call letters to WKNR.)

The station was owned by Fred and Nellie Knorr; that's where the KNR came from. The programmers of the Detroit station set up the Battle Creek station and used it as kind of a farm team to develop talent for the big time in the Motor City.

So the story goes: WELL in Battle Creek was a boring, middle-of-the-road music station when the decision was made, after WKNR in Detroit became wildly popular playing rock and roll, to switch the Battle Creek station to do the same thing.

The Detroit programmers were in Battle Creek trying to figure out what the new call letters would be. General Manager Kent Kanaga said, "It's got to sound like Keener or mean Keener."

And someone else said, "Hey, you're at fourteen hundred on the dial; how about KFR, which will stand for Keener Fourteen?" So Keener 14 was born. That happened in 1964; when 1970 rolled around, Keener 14 would get a new news director, soon to become program director.

Barry Newman moved from WREO in Ashtabula to Keener in Battle Creek and told them about me. They invited me in for an interview. I got in the door because a friend recommended me for the job, again!

The Michigan National Bank building in Battle Creek was located at the corner of Michigan and Capital Avenues. Sadly, when Ruth and I returned in 2009, the building had been torn down. Back then, though, Keener was on the seventh floor; I was looking for suite 710. I found it, and when I walked through the door, I immediately ran into a partition, allowing me only about two feet of standing room as I looked into the main office. It was small—really small. A woman nearby let out a sigh, slammed down the papers on her desk got up and asked, "Can I help you?"

"I'm here to see the program director, Bob Absher," I answered.

Bob was sitting right there in front of me at a desk on the other side of the partition, about four feet away. She looked at him, and he looked at me and with his hose high in the air, arrogantly said, "Yes?"

"I'm Rick D'Amico."

"Come in," he said. I walked around the partition, and he walked me back to the studios. We passed through a sales office and into a dirty room with two humming transmitters and a Coke machine, and then into a tiny production studio.

He showed me around. Across from the production studio was a tiny news booth and then the main control room. It was a crappy station equipment-wise, reminiscent of WWGO in Erie, Pennsylvania—old equipment and shabby walls, and it was just ugly. He took me back to the general manager's office. The GM had a big office—wood-paneled with a huge desk and big executive chair—and sitting in the chair was Kent Kanaga.

Mr. Kanaga was a nice man, chubby and bald. He was dark-skinned with kind eyes behind horn-rimmed glasses. I liked him immediately. He was management, but I liked him! I was hired to be the new news director at $125 a week, or $6,500 a year. Not exactly the fifty grand I could have made at the *Cleveland Plain Dealer*, but I was happy.

Ruth and I packed our bags, and we made the trek from Ohio to Michigan with our newborn.

My first day on the job was a little hectic. I was in the newsroom trying to figure out what the equipment was all about, what kind of state Michigan was, and what Battle Creek was all about, when Absher walked in with a young man wearing sneakers and a casual sport coat.

"Rick, this is Sander Levin," he said. "He's running for governor of Michigan!"

"How do you do?" I said.

Absher offered him a seat in the production studio, and I put on a tape and began an interview. Now, this was my first day on the job. I had just moved in from Ohio. I had no idea who he was or what the politics were all about—I didn't even know if he was a Democrat or a Republican. I said, "This is my first day on the job."

He smiled and answered, "No problem. This is my first time running for governor!" We hit it off immediately.

With a lump in my throat, I began. "Mr. Levin, what are the issues of this campaign?" Levin went on to talk for about twenty minutes. I got what I needed and thanked him. Levin was very kind and gracious.

Levin lost the election to William Milliken. But as I write this, Levin is an esteemed member of Congress, representing the Twelfth Congressional

District of Michigan, and is the brother of longtime senator Carl Levin. During joint sessions of Congress, I would see him sitting next to his brother, and I was always reminded of my first day on the job as a fledgling radio newsman in Battle Creek.

The Keener news department consisted of three people: me; afternoon newsman Otis Buchannan; and a blind man, Ed Barnes, who sat at home and listened to the police scanners and called us with news tips.

One of my duties as news director was to cover the city-council meetings. Sometimes they would last late into the night. I would go back to the station with my notes (which were indecipherable) to write the story and try to be accurate, honest, and fair. Many times I thought, *Our audience is depending on me and only me to report the truth!* It was an awesome responsibility. I did not take it lightly.

Although Battle Creek was a small town, it had big-city problems and huge stories. For example, the Kellogg strike, the police strike, race riots, accusations that Kellogg cereals were not nutritious, Cedar Point announcing it was going to build a giant amusement park in Battle Creek and later canceling, and plenty of armed robberies and police shootings. It was a real change from covering the county sheriff in Ashtabula, where someone might have been thrown in jail for stealing a chicken.

My air shift anchoring newscasts was from sign-on at 5:00 a.m. to about 4:00 p.m., and then there would be late nights covering city council and other stories. It was really challenging.

Every morning, the program director would call me before we went on the air at 5:00 a.m. to ask what the stories were. I also had the responsibility of covering West Michigan for the Associated Press (AP). After reporting to the boss, I would also have to file stories with the AP. On the phone, they would drill me. "Who says?" they would ask. "Where, what, when, why, how, who, and again according to whom?" Every time I would read a story on TV in Phoenix some forty-five years later, these questions would ring in my mind. Sadly, the news writers of today can't even come close to this discipline. I believe many of them may not even know the meaning of the word *attribution*.

When the Battle Creek police officers went on strike, I covered the story as a street reporter and spent time on the picket lines interviewing cops. I would rush back to the station, write the stories, edit the sound bites, and anchor newscasts.

One day, a county deputy sheriff appeared at the office and asked for me. "Rick D'Amico?"

"Yes, that's me," I answered. He handed me a subpoena! It said I was to appear in court and present all my notes and taped interviews of the striking officers.

I immediately reported this on the air. "This is purely in violation of the First Amendment to the Constitution of the United States," I announced, "and I'll go to jail before I give up my notes."

So there I was appearing in a courtroom before the judge, ready to go to jail. Proceedings began, and the judge said, "I'm so sorry for the subpoena. These forms have my signature stamped on them, and I had no intention of the court taking your notes and tapes. I apologize, Mr. D'Amico."

As it turns out, the judge had been inundated with letters and phone calls from news directors and reporters from across the nation protesting the subpoena. Sadly, today this would not happen; most courts, in recent years, have trampled on the freedom of the press.

■ ■ ■

But it wasn't all serious journalism: there were some bizarre, hilarious, and almost unbelievable things that happened at Keener Radio.

Jim Robinson was the afternoon DJ, and I guess he was a lone wolf, a free spirit. One day, while sitting in the newsroom, which overlooked the control room, I looked up. Jim was sitting behind the mike doing his shift. Then I looked down and looked up again, and he was gone. I never saw him again. He had been fired; I don't know why. He was immediately replaced by DJ Mike Scott.

Paul Harvey News and Comment, broadcast coast to coast on the ABC Radio Network, was one of the most important programs on the station.

It offered GM Kanaga a bit of prestige, and the sponsors of Harvey were always extremely important. One of my duties was to record Harvey and play it back after the noon news. God help you if you missed it. But one day I did—I missed it. If Harvey didn't play, there was hell to pay!

So I called WKMI radio in Kalamazoo, Michigan, and asked if I could patch them into our station when they played Harvey. They agreed. I patched them in, and Harvey began as if nothing had gone wrong, but then something terrible happened.

About ten minutes into the Harvey broadcast, the disgruntled Jim Robinson called into the station to complain to Mike Scott about being fired. How it happened, I don't know, but in the process of patching in Harvey, the phone line was also patched in! And Robinson let loose, using every four-letter word he could think of, including the f-word, screaming into the phone a number of times, and yes, that was going over the air along with *Paul Harvey News and Comment.*

The phone lines lit up. One of the ladies in the office came running back to the control room and screamed at Mike Scott, "Somebody is swearing on the air, during Paul Harvey," as if it were sacrilegious! And, by the way, it was.

Mike Scott said in the phone, "Hold on, Jim," and he turned up the speaker and heard Harvey and, of course, Jim Robinson was silent, waiting for Scott to come back on the phone.

Scott didn't hear anything unusual and said, "I don't hear anything." He went back to his conversation with Robinson—and the four-letter words continued! This went on for about five minutes until there were more complaints—and more four-letter words—but finally, Scott hung up with Robinson, and I figured out that I had done something wrong when patching in Harvey.

No one was fired, but we were all really scared. Still, afterward, we were laughing our butts off, obviously! And nothing came of it—no fines from the FCC, no repercussions from Harvey's network, just unbelievable memories.

At the time, my heart was not in news. I wanted to be the program director, and Absher was not very popular with the staff. He was a former news reporter and didn't particularly like or know Top 40 radio. Kanaga called me into the office one day out of the blue and asked if I would be the program director, and I wholeheartedly accepted. Absher left soon after that, and I had the task of moving Keener into the seventies sound of "More Music Top 40 Radio."

It was the time of my life. I put together a station that emphasized music and minimized clutter, and I believed it sounded like a major-market Top 40 radio station, with a super staff of radio personalities.

Because it was a small station that didn't pay very much, there was the usual parade of DJs who came through the station while I was there. It is difficult to remember them all, but here are some of the standouts.

You can count on the fingers of one hand the truly talented, funny radio personalities who are out there. And Bill Gray comes in at the top of the list. Bill was our morning man. The all-important drive-time morning shift brought in the most dough from advertisers, and you needed a strong talent to fill the bill, and Bill was the bill!

I can't begin to tell you how funny this man was and how funny he continues to be to this very day. I got a feeling of joy and happiness just listening to his morning banter. We were lucky to have him.

Bill liked to play pranks on the other DJs at the station. For example, one of the features I instituted was the "Keener Secret Word." This was nothing more than the name of a citizen we would announce throughout the day. "Today's Keener Secret Word is John Smith!" It would get people talking. Some days Bill would change the name temporarily to something like Al Kaholic.

The next jock would say, without even knowing what he was saying, "Al Kaholic!" Another one of my favorites was "Dick Hurtz." Meanwhile, we all gathered in the production studio listening and laughing like crazy. Bill continued his radio career working on WBCK in Battle Creek for over thirty years before retiring in 2009. To this day, the funniest comments I get on my Facebook page are from Bill.

Dick DeYoung was a wonderful guy. He was very intellectual; he was also a smooth-talking, mellow personality and a good friend. While I was in the studio with him during his air shift, he would occasionally turn on the mike switch but keep the volume off, and he would say something like "This next song will knock the dew off your penis!"

I would gasp. "What did you just say?" He would laugh and say the mike was off. He caught me a number of times doing that.

Dick's family and my family were close; we had children the same age, and we spent a lot of time together. Dick passed away in 2012.

Dave Hoppe was just out of high school in Battle Creek and was our best Top 40 performer—he was young and talented and ran a good show. Dave was very popular. He was our music director and helped me program the station. To this day we keep in touch.

Gary Malernee was the son of a very successful dentist in town, and I think that made Gary a little crazy. He was bold and outrageous and funny and obnoxious, and everybody loved him. Gary also did the commercials for Jury Rowe Furniture. He would scream his head off, and Jury Rowe made a lot of money out of it.

One day, I was doing a live broadcast from Jury Rowe Furniture, and Malernee came to me with a broken-down lamp that actually had part of the base broken off. "Hey, Rick, say on the air that the next person who comes in the store gets a free lamp."

I said, "Are you kidding? You want to give away that piece of crap?"

"Try it!" he said.

So I did. A few minutes later, a car came crashing through the window of the store. Glass was falling all over the place, and the driver screamed, "Do I get the lamp?"

And I'll never forget Roy LaFountain, mostly because we had something in common. Roy walked in one day and said he wanted to be on the air. The first thing he said was, as he was motioning like he was taking a swing with a baseball bat, "Just got back from a softball game."

"You play softball?"

"Yeah, I love it."

"Do you have any radio experience?" I asked.

"No, but everybody says I have a good voice for radio," he answered.

I hired him to run the control board during the Detroit Tigers games on our FM. Roy eventually made it to the Keener Air staff and was very good, but he had a similar problem to the one I had with broadcast equipment.

One of Roy's shifts was Sunday morning sign-on. Similar to my first job in radio, Roy's job was to play some music in between the religious shows. On one Sunday morning, it was time for the live broadcast from a local church. Roy would patch in the feed from the church, and the church members would take over with their Sunday morning worship services.

As the services began, the organ music started, and the pastor began his opening prayer. I was listening to make sure Roy had done everything right. While the pastor was praying, I heard Roy's voice saying, "Hello, test; hello, test; hello, testes, testing, testes, penis, penis." Over and over again!

Roy was in the production studio, and he had patched both the church and the production studio on the air, so without his knowing it, his lewd remarks were going over the air at the same time the preacher was praying. Mine wasn't the first call to get through; the state police got through first, and then hundreds of listeners! By time I got to him, he was in a sheer panic.

Roy went on to be an amazing talent and is still on the air in Battle Creek on WBCK.

Kevin Sanderson was a high-school student who came to the station once a week to pick up a load of our Tunedexes—the Keener Top 30, our published record charts—for his church's teen dance. Then he wouldn't leave; he would just start hanging around the station—so I put him to work! Kevin went on to Detroit radio and is still on the air today. He is, among other things, the traffic reporter for the Fox TV station in Detroit, WJBK-TV.

Doak Breen came in one day to ask for a job, and his voice was so wonderful, I hired him immediately. He's on the air today in Detroit on WWJ. Jim Hawke was another outstanding news anchor who had a deep voice; he went on to work in Washington, DC.

Vaughn Royal was a fantastic afternoon DJ who went on to become a successful attorney in our nation's capital.

The Keener radio jocks were fun-loving and happy-go-lucky. They loved the station, the town, and the music types of personalities. They were having fun, which was the presentation and the legacy of the past that they lived up to.

But then came Matt Majewski. Matt was different. Matt's on-air personality was sarcastic, cruel, and angry, but he was just hilarious. He shocked the town and, I might add, the boss. Matt would make fun of the city, the audience, even the mayor—anywhere he found humor.

One day he was talking about the mayor, and he yelled into the microphone, "Mayor, eat my shorts!"

I thought Kent Kanaga was going to have a heart attack. He had never heard a DJ say anything like that. He called me into his office. "That's dirty!" he cried.

"Well, now, I don't know that it's really dirty or even bad. All he said was 'eat my shorts'; it could mean anything." I tried to defend him as much as I could.

"I don't like him; he's mean," Kanaga said.

"I know, but it's kind of like Don Rickles," I said. "It's humor." And Matt was really good at it.

My method of dealing with air talent was not to punish, but to encourage them to be creative and to be big personalities. I tried not to criticize, but to come up with ideas on how to make them better and to be different.

Needless to say, I spent a lot of time in Kanaga's office talking about Matt. Matt went on to work major markets, including Houston and Phoenix; he was an outstanding talent. He was on the air on KEZ-FM when I arrived in Phoenix in 1987.

And the news people—wow, what a staff! Joe Landon was one of the hardest-working news directors I've ever worked with. Joe was a strong family man, and he and his family went camping a lot on weekends, so he traded in his family car for a camper and actually drove his camper to work.

And there was Matt McLogan, a very bright, young, articulate man who was one of our best news directors. He went on to serve the state of Michigan as a public-service commissioner and today is the vice president for university relations of Grand Valley State University in Allendale, Michigan.

Next, Suzie Geha was one of the most wonderful broadcasters I had the honor of working with. It was a challenge on my part to hire her. This is how it came about. Our afternoon news anchor—the fourth or fifth one we'd had while I was there—had abruptly left the station. News director Matt McLogan was given the assignment to hire somebody, with my approval. "There is one person who would be perfect for the job," he told me.

"Who?" I asked.

"Her name is Suzanne Geha."

"That's impossible," I said. "Kanaga would never allow a woman on the staff!" This was 1971.

Kent Kanaga, the general manager, was, as I said before, a nice guy, but to be truthful, he really didn't have a clue as to what was going on. He lived in his own world of lunches at the Athelstan Club in the Security National Bank Building and dinners at the Battle Creek Country Club.

Kanaga used one of those two-pages-per-day calendars on his desk. On the right side of the calendar, he would write, very small, his agenda for the day. When he accomplished a task, he would draw a line through it.

Every morning before he arrived for work, I would sneak into his office and take a look. If I saw a problem or issue on that list that dealt with programming, something I didn't want to deal with, or perhaps that I thought was ridiculous, I would just cross it off the list. He would come into work, see it crossed off, figure it had already been done, and forget about it—honest!

One Monday morning, he called me into his office with a problem not on his calendar. "We don't seem to be having any contests on the air." He looked at me with a worried look.

"Kent, just this past weekend, we gave away over a thousand dollars in prizes in the Coca-Cola giveaway," I said.

He looked confused. "Oh." That was the conversation!

Almost every afternoon at around 3:00 p.m., he would leave for the day. On the way home, he would stop and get an ice-cream cone. If I wanted him to approve something, I would approach him at around 2:50 p.m. He was in a hurry to get that cone! "Kent, we really need to get a new jingle package," I said once.

Impatiently, he asked, "How much?"

"I don't know, around three or four thousand dollars."

"Geesh, I don't know." But the thought of that ice-cream cone was taking over his mind. He got flustered. I just looked at him, knowing he didn't have a chance; the craving for that cone was intense. "Oh, just do what you want!" he cried as he ran out of the station. That's how I got things done.

Early on, we had a newsman named Otis Buchannan. Otis was African American. Kent thought if we upset him in any way, the NAACP would boycott the station. He would regularly call me into his office, close the door, lower his voice, and ask, "How's Otis doing?"

"Just fine," I would answer.

"You have to be nice to him, you know, because he's…"—and then he would whisper—"black!"

"I know. He's a good man," I would say.

So getting back to hiring Suzie Geha. Matt McLogan had this young lady, about to graduate from Western Michigan University in Kalamazoo. She was McLogan's pick for our new afternoon news anchor. She came in for an audition and blew me away.

Suzie Geha was bright, beautiful, energetic, and engaging. She was fabulous on the air, she was an excellent writer, and she loved the news. She made a tape, and I was waiting for the right time to play it for Kanaga.

He was leaving for a two-week trip to Florida in his motor home. He called me into his office. "Say, Rick, have you found a newsman yet?" he asked.

"I got someone who is just right for the job."

"Who is he?"

"Well, it's not a he; it's a she," I said.

"Oh no! Oh my God! You can't hire a woman!" he exclaimed.

"Why not?"

"Because women, women, they have, they have, problems!" he said as he contorted his face and looked like he had broken out into a sweat. I dropped the topic. He left for two weeks.

While he was gone, I hired her. Two weeks later, he came back from vacation. First thing on his agenda, he called me into his office. "Say, Rick, Phillis [his wife] and I were driving back from Florida yesterday, and we were listening to the station, and the afternoon newsman kind of sounds like a girl!"

"That's because she *is* a girl. Suzanne Geha—isn't she wonderful?" I asked.

He put his hands on the sides of his head, blocking his ears, so he couldn't hear anything else I had to say; then he swiveled around in his big executive chair, with his back facing me. He gazed out the window, and I left his office. He didn't talk to me for two weeks.

I don't know when during that two-week period it happened—perhaps it was the positive feedback he was getting from his friends at the country club—but it did happen: he decided Suzie Geha was the best thing that ever happened to the station. He just loved her.

Suzanne Geha went on to distinguish herself, not only as one of the first female newscasters in Michigan but also as one of the most beloved and popular news anchors in all of west Michigan. She anchored prime time on WOOD-TV in Grand Rapids for over thirty years. She also spent time anchoring the news on WXYZ in Detroit.

After Suzie left, Kanaga said, "We have to replace her with a woman." My, how things changed! The female-newscaster glass ceiling at Keener had been broken. We hired Barbara Marineau. She was awesome, but her dreams were to become an actress. Years later, she showed up on TV's *Law and Order* and on Broadway.

■ ■ ■

One dirty little secret that Keener DJs had was only revealed some thirty years later, at the Keener reunion: The Coke machine next to the transmitters had a secret button on the side. You pushed the button, and out came a Coke—for free! On our salaries, this was a big deal. DJ Dave Thomas revealed this at the reunion dinner party and asked how many in the audience had known about it. I immediately shot up my hand and looked around, and I was the only one. Everyone laughed.

Our sales staff at Keener consisted of two energetic, money-loving guys: John Gamin, who was replaced later by Dick Steimonoff, and Wally Ahlers. Wally was known as "Mr. Keener." Wally walked around town all decked out in white shoes, a matching white belt, and an umbrella, even when it wasn't raining.

Wally was the best at what he did. For him, radio was all about selling commercials and getting those commercials on the air, and heaven help anyone who screwed it up. One day, something happened when a jock missed some of his commercials. Wally ran into the studio, took out his wallet, and said, "See this? What do I need this for?" And he threw it on the floor. "If you guys don't play my spots, I don't make any money!"

Remember "Play the spots!" from my first day on the air on Johnny Reb Radio in Albany, Georgia?

And you know something, if Wally didn't get paid, neither did anyone else, for our livelihood depended on Wally and the other sales guys to bring in the bucks. I love Wally; he was one of the true legends of our little station. We keep in touch, and when he visits Phoenix during the winter, he and his wife, Alta, and Ruth and I always make it a point to get together for lunch.

I had always admired Wally because I thought he was making a lot of money, and I entertained the thought of going into sales. Kanaga decided to take our FM in a different direction. Instead of simulcasting our AM, our FM would become an automated, beautiful music station, called "The Beautiful Island." And I would be the sales manager.

When the big day came, I arrived for work in a suit and tie, walked into Kanaga's office, and said, "Well, here I am; what do I do?"

"Oh," Kanaga said, "you just go into a store and ask if they want to buy some spots." Some advice this was. I went to see Wally.

"Hey, go down to the Firestone store and see Mr. Dana; he loves your FM station!"

Wow, I thought, *this is going to be easy.* The Firestone store was on the main drag, Michigan Avenue. I walked in, saw a man in a Firestone uniform, and said, "Mr. Dana?"

"Yes?" he said.

"I'm Rick D'Amico, from WKFR-FM, the Beautiful Island!" I exclaimed.

"Get the hell out of here, and never come back!" he yelled.

I walked out of there with my tail between my legs and went back into the Keener sales office.

"What did he say?" Wally asked.

"He threw me out of the store!" I cried.

"Yeah," Wally said, laughing, "he does that to everyone."

So this was my introduction to sales.

As you can see, my time at Keener 14 in Battle Creek was all about learning the business of broadcasting hands-on. I learned that to have a successful business, it takes all people working together to be responsible for the entire operation; we all had a hand in its success. It was an entrepreneurial endeavor, and we all cared. This environment does not exist in broadcasting today. Most radio and TV stations are owned by big corporations, and for the most part, people just do their jobs, collect a paycheck, and hope to get out alive.

After two years at Keener, I found Ruth, our baby daughter, and myself living on a tropical island. How that happened is next.

10

WBMJ, SAN JUAN, PUERTO RICO, A BOB HOPE STATION

"Don't you speak Spanish?" He had a disgusted
look on his face.
"Me? No, I'm from Cleveland; I'm Italian!"

In 1972, my third year in Battle Creek, Bill Gray was just back from the Virgin Islands. He had left for an adventure: to work at a radio station in the Caribbean. It was his dream job. After a couple of years, it was time for him to come home, and we hired him back in a heartbeat.

Bill and I would spend hours talking about living on a tropical island. He told me about living on a sailboat, taking a dinghy into shore to go to his radio job, and spending hours on the beach. It was my dream! I'd always wanted a sailboat and always wanted to live in a warm climate. Most of these conversations took place in the dead of a Michigan winter, when it was cloudy, gray, cold, snowy, and depressing. Needless to say, I was motivated; if only that dream could come true.

Bill raved about the big powerhouse radio station in the Caribbean owned by Bob Hope, WBMJ in San Juan, Puerto Rico. He said it was the station to work for; it was big time, had lots of money, and could be heard all throughout the Caribbean. Bill said that every hour on the half hour, an announcer would say, "You're listening to WBMJ, San Juan, Puerto Rico, a Bob Hope Station!" And then, as Bill described it, "A jingle would play—'Thanks for the Memories,' Bob Hope's theme song—and then an oldie. It was amazing." Bill had me. I would give anything to work there.

I prayed, "Lord, someday, I would love to work there." And guess what? A few months later, a miracle happened!

I was in the radio station, looking out the seventh-floor window down on some of the buildings of downtown Battle Creek. It was a cold, gray morning; snow and ice covered parts of the tar paper on the roofs, and on the streets, week-old snow had turned black and was piled high on the street corners. I grabbed a *Broadcasting* magazine and immediately went to the back, where the job openings were listed. I said a prayer: "Lord, please get me a job in the Caribbean." I got to the section where the DJ openings were, and there it was, an ad that said, "Wanted, Radio Personality for WBMJ in San Juan. Send tape and résumé."

"Thank you, Lord!"

I put an air check, a recording of one of my air shifts, and a résumé in the mail; said a prayer; and sent it off.

Not long after that, I got a call from San Juan, Puerto Rico, from WBMJ. The program director's name was Mike Michaels.

"Do you have any relatives living here?" he asked.

Oh no, not that question again! "No," I answered.

"Are you married?"

"Yes, with one child," I answered.

"Good," he said. This information sold him on hiring me; the reason will be revealed later. "You got the job; how soon can you be here?" he asked.

"Well, gee whiz, a couple of weeks, maybe a month; I have to sell some things."

"Great," he said, "keep in touch."

Puerto Rico in 1972 was, as it is today, a territory of the United States, not a state, nor a foreign country, so traveling there requires no passport and living there requires no visa. There were no taxes—either sales or income—at the time; however, there were some other important differences. One was there were too many cars, so they had a hefty import excise tax on all cars coming into the island. I had two cars I had to sell before moving there.

I also had a mobile home to sell—not an easy thing to do. And then there were all the winter clothes to get rid of. Year-round, the average temperature on the island is about eighty degrees, so there's no need for the heavy Michigan parkas and sweaters. Ruth and I did everything we could to get rid of just about all we had.

So finally the day came. Dick DeYoung had a going-away party for us at his house, and all the Keener air staff was there. The next morning, we flew to Cleveland to spend a few days with my family, and we caught a flight to San Juan.

Ruth; my two-year-old daughter, Michelle; and I schlepped all of what was left of our worldly belongings on that Eastern Airlines plane and took off for Miami, where the plane made a brief stop. The flight was uneventful except for one incident. Michelle was two, and she was potty-trained, and she had to go to the bathroom. She was afraid to go to the airplane restroom, so Ruth pulled out her potty chair and assembled it in the aisle, and there was little Michelle going potty in the aisle.

When the plane stopped in Miami, I noticed something different. Most people got off, and the plane loaded up with people from Puerto Rico on their way home. It was just crowded, with every seat full, which was unusual in those days. And everyone seemed to be happy and full of life. I was feeling good.

As the plane approached Puerto Rico, I looked down and saw the ocean, the palm trees, and the beaches, and I was ecstatic.

Munoz International Airport, at the time, was an open-air airport, with open-air terminals. We stepped off the plane, and the humidity slapped us right in the face! Ruth looked at me in shock. It was hot and wet, but I thought, *I'm in paradise at last.*

The general manager was to meet us at the airport. As we walked toward the terminal, a young man, probably in his thirties, with a full-face beard, who was kind of scraggly looking, was standing there wearing a sport shirt. Attached to one of his pockets, I noticed a WBMJ patch. *It's my new boss waiting to welcome us to paradise*, I thought.

I walked over to him and said, "I'm Rick D'Amico!"

"I'm Bob Bennett. ¡Hola!"

"'Hola'—what does that mean?" I replied.

His smile turned to a frown. "Don't you speak Spanish?" He had a disgusted look on his face.

"Me? No, I'm from Cleveland; I'm Italian!"

"Oh no," he replied. This was the beginning of something I thought was not so good.

Bob Bennett, an alumnus of the famed Storz Broadcasting Company, was the station general manager. He drove us around the neighborhoods, showing us the town and where we might want to live. I looked up at a street sign I was trying to read. "Ca-lee Taft?" I asked.

"Cal-yay!" he corrected me. "Really, you don't speak Spanish?"

"Uh-uh," I sadly replied in the negative.

He showed us around the station; it was beautiful. Located in the penthouse of the Borinquin Hotel overlooking San Juan Bay, the windows of the studios had a beautiful view of the bay; a cruise ship was coming into to port, and all the equipment was first-class and brand-new.

He gave me two keys to the station. "This one is for the front door, and this one is for the gate," he explained.

"What's the gate?" I asked.

"The gate closes in front of the door; it's to keep the Independentistas from bombing the station again!"

"What?" Ruth's eyes were bulging out of their sockets.

"Well, you see, there is this group of people who don't want Puerto Rico to have anything to do with the United States, and they hate us being an American-owned radio station, so one time they threw a bomb past the front door! It didn't go off."

Oh, *that* was comforting.

■ ■ ■

This was the beginning of our adventure in the Caribbean. We stayed in the Borinquin Hotel until we found a nice apartment to rent in the Condado, a touristy area in Santurce that had the feel of Miami. It was about a half block from the beach. It had no air conditioning, but the windows went from ceiling to floor and opened wide to the constant winds blowing through the apartment. It was refreshing and open-air, like most buildings there.

I quickly got promoted to the morning shift, but I had this problem: I did not speak Spanish. They assigned the sales manager to teach me the pronunciation of the Spanish vowels. So at least I could pronounce words, even if I didn't understand them.

Now, I should point out that most people in Puerto Rico speak Spanish. English may be the secondary language, but most people prefer Spanish. And while WBMJ at the time was an English-speaking station, many of the commercials were in Spanish, and most people you dealt with on the phones and in person spoke Spanish. This was a real challenge.

One morning, we were doing a promotion called "The WBMJ Lovebug Contest." You had to be the correct caller; for example, if I asked for caller number four, you had to be the fourth caller on the line, and if so, you won two lovebug patches and were eligible to win a Volkswagen. I put on a Michael Jackson record that was about two-and-a-half minutes long and then said, "I'll take the tenth caller on the WBMJ Love Line to win two free lovebug patches and be eligible to win a Volkswagen Beetle—call now!" When I got to the tenth caller, I said in the phone, while the record was playing, "You're the tenth caller—you win! What's your name?"

The voice on the other end of the phone said something like, "Jose Martin Gonzales Sosa de Roche."

"What?" I panicked.

"Jose...Martin...Gonzales...Sosa de Roche." he said.

"Oh my God, can you please spell that?" He did. "What's your address?"

"Uno dos cuatro ocho Calle Venecia, Bayamon, Puerto Rico."

"Oh my God." My record ran out, and there was dead air—the record was over, the needle was playing the label, and I was totally embarrassed.

I would occasionally get Spanish and English pronunciations confused, pronouncing English words as if they were in Spanish; it was just a nightmare. "Our team is having a blast down at the sta-dee-oom—or is that 'stadium'?"

Most of the commercials were in Spanish, and the out cues were labeled on the tape cartridges. *"Ahora mismo"* was the out cue. I was waiting for it, but I missed it—dead air. What a mess.

Ruth would take our daughter, Michelle, who was two years old, into a restaurant and order something to drink for the baby, and they would bring a beer; it was hilarious.

The phone would ring, and I would pick up the phone and not say a thing. The voice on the other end would say, "¡Hola!"

I would say, "I'm from Cleveland; please speak English."

One day, after living without television, we decided to go to the mall and buy a TV. Plaza las Americas looked like any mall in the United States. We found JC Penney, but I wasn't going to be fooled. I knew that although around here everything looked American, everybody spoke Spanish. I walked up to a salesman and said, "Televisioney?...el televisor? We want to buy a televisioney!" and then I made a gesture with my hands of what I thought might tip him off that what I wanted to buy was a television.

He said, "Now, do you want to buy a television?"

"Oh yes!" I was relived.

We got the TV home and plugged it in, and *Bonanza* was on. Here came Hoss and Little Joe and Pa, riding up on their horses. Then Hoss spoke. "¡Buenas noches!" It was all in Spanish! The only show in English that we found was *Sesame Street*.

There were days when we would be on the beach and I would look at my watch and say to Ruth, "Honey, if we leave now, we can get back home just in time to watch *Sesame Street*. I wonder what Burt and Ernie are up to."

When we decided to leave San Juan, I had the hardest time trying to cancel the paper with the paperboy. "I'm leaving; I no longer need the paper."

"Huh?"

"Moving back to Michigan."

"Huh?"

Then my voice got louder. "No more paper! Going back to the United States, no paper—no more!" I was screaming at the top of my lungs, as if the louder I got, the more likely it was that he would understand me. Neighbors in the building came rushing into the hallway and heard me yelling.

One hysterical lady came running into the hallway. "¿Qué pasa?"

I looked at her in desperation. "I'm going home; I don't want the paper anymore." She made the translation for me.

One morning while I was walking to the bus station, a police officer stopped me and asked, "Do you have the time?"

My brain scrambled between English and Spanish; I accidentally replied, "I don't speak English."

While I was doing the morning show, I pulled out all the stops, using all my one-liners and jokes. I thought I was funny. After my shift one morning, the general manager called me into his office. "You are definitely one of the funniest morning personalities we've ever had on the air here; you really are funny," he said. "But I have a bit of advice for you."

"What's that?"

"Don't tell jokes."

"Why not?"

He looked at me and said, "Our audience doesn't understand English!"

Was this perfect for me? I don't think so!

There were mornings when I was all alone and the wires would signal a bulletin. I would rush into the newsroom, and the bulletin would be in Spanish. I thought, *The world could be coming to an end, and I have no idea what's going on.*

Twice every half hour, we had to play a record from what the program director called "the Latino lineup." It was a song by a Puerto Rican artist. When I played one of these songs, the native Puerto Ricans in the office would jump into the hallway and dance. It was a riot.

The DJs would come to work in swim trunks and swim in the hotel pool during their breaks. The next time you're listening to the radio, picture the DJ talking to you in a Speedo.

There were two on-air personalities whom I remember. One was news director George MacDougle. He looked like David Crosby of Crosby, Stills, and Nash—the same hair.

Marty Malo came on after me. He was a fast-talking, very talented DJ who went on to become a very successful major-market television news anchor. His real name was Mike Hambrick. Mike had two brothers, John and Judd, two major-market TV news anchors who were big personalities in my hometown of Cleveland, Ohio.

After being promoted to the morning show, I felt I needed a car, rather than take the bus to work, which would save me a lot of time, so I decided to buy a car. This was an experience right out of the movie *The In-Laws* with Peter Falk and Alan Arkin.

The sales manager took me to a used-car dealer, and the entire deal between him and the salesman was consummated in Spanish; I had no idea what was happening. At times they were getting into a heated argument with each other, yelling like crazy. It was all in Spanish. I just sat there smiling. The car salesman looked at me and said something in Spanish, and I would sheepishly nod my head in agreement.

The car was a used Volkswagen. The sales manager said, "It's a good car, perfect for San Juan, and you got a good deal." It was orange, with four Puerto Rico stickers on it—two on the front fenders and two on the back fenders. When we sold the car to move back to Michigan, the new owners took the stickers off, and underneath were bullet holes! When the new owners drove up to the mountains, the brakes failed.

Selling the car was also a scream. About four months after we bought the car, we decided to move back Michigan. That was a real problem, seeing it took at least a year to get the title. Things moved slowly there. So the car buyer's boyfriend, who was studying to be a lawyer, said he had a lot of connections, and he took us to a high-rise office building, where there was this guy in a suit. *Must be some government official*, I thought. The entire deal was done, once again, in Spanish. Ruth and I just sat there and smiled, nodding. We thought everything was taken care of.

For months after we returned to Michigan, we received citations and court orders to appear in San Juan for traffic violations. To this day, I don't really know if that car is still in my name.

After working there a few weeks, it was explained to me that the station was forced to hire DJs who were married, because single guys had a hard time living on the island because they could not assimilate into the culture. Guys with wives and children were able to cope.

One day, after about four months at the station, kindhearted Kent Kanaga, the Keener Radio general manager in Battle Creek, Michigan, called me and said, "Just consider your stay there a vacation; I will send you the money to fly back to Michigan." And this is what we did.

11

"HELLO DARE, MAMA!"

*A tall African American man was standing be-
hind his screen door in his jockey shorts. He
looked at her and said, "Hello dare, mama!"*

We returned to Battle Creek in the fall, with only three trunks of our
stuff—mostly warm-weather clothes. We checked into a downtown motel
and later found what we thought was a nice apartment, where the rent was
really cheap. Turns out it was a rent-subsidized apartment complex, which
presented its own set of challenges.

One day while we watched TV, seven police officers ran by my living-
room window with rifles drawn! It was a raid on one of the apartments;
this was a high-crime area. We had to be careful getting in and out of our
cars and into our house.

I'll never forget one day when Ruth was walking from our car to our
apartment, and a tall African-American man was standing behind his
screen door in his jockey shorts. He looked at her and said, "Hello dare,
mama!" This became my expression every time I saw a good-looking girl.
I used it on the air on TV some forty years later, and it kind of became one
of my trademark expressions.

The next four years became some of the happiest days of my career. I was programming the Keener Radio, and it was my vision of what a Top 40 station should be.

We broke a lot of records, meaning we were the first to play records that would become hits. Record-promotion people from Detroit would visit and depend on us to get airplay so that Detroit radio would be convinced to also play the records. Motown artists would stop by the station, as well as other rock stars. One day Paul Revere of Paul Revere and the Raiders stopped in while riding his motorcycle to Detroit. He just wanted to talk! Many Motown stars would just walk in to be on our shows. Jackey Beavers, who wrote the Diana Ross hit "Someday We'll Be Together," used to stop by all the time with his good friend Junior Walker. One day I was sitting at my desk when the door opened, and it was Don Gardner of "I Need Your Lovin' Every Day." He said, "Just stopped in to say hello!"

Keener 14 was well respected as a legendary little radio station.

We also were one the first stations in the country to play *American Top 40*, the syndicated Top 40 countdown show hosted by Casey Kasem. Working there was just a dream come true—until one terrible thing happened.

The DJs were unhappy about their pay, and one day someone got the bright idea to go union.

Being in management, I was dead set against it. I knew how these things worked in radio; by the time all the dust settled, the people who started the whole thing would have moved on, leaving a mess behind.

The Grain Millers—yes, the Grain Millers—union (this is Battle Creek, Michigan, remember) made the initial contact with Kanaga, and all hell broke loose.

While negotiations were going on, Kanaga would meet with his managers in his office to discuss his strategy. Now, here's the funny part. Kanaga's office was also used as a studio for a weekly public-affairs program, and on his conference table were two or three microphones that were connected to the production studio. While he discussed what he was going to do to break the union, the DJs would gather in the production studio and listen in.

This was a very dark time in the history of Keener Radio. I found myself in the middle of a very rancorous fight between management and staff. I was deeply devoted to the air staff, but also to General Manager Kanaga, and I knew what both sides were doing, but couldn't share the information with either. Kanaga took the drastic step of automating Keener 14 AM and eliminating the air staff. It was really sad.

By this time Keener FM had become an automated station, and Kanaga had me fly to Santa Barbara, California, to order automation equipment for the AM. The automation equipment arrived—big reel-to-reel tape players and tape-cart machines—and most of the DJs had to leave or be fired. The union was busted. Keener, by the way, was the first station in the United States to play the automated Drake-Chenault format of XT-40.

After working in television for more than thirty years, I could not help but notice that TV was doing the same thing: automating anything it could. During my last few years in television, a great number of people at the station were eliminated by automation and consolidation. It's interesting to me how TV seems to follow its parent radio in just about everything from programming to engineering.

Bill Gray, the guy who had sold me on moving to Puerto Rico, and I kept in touch. By this time, he was selling classified ads for the *Battle Creek Enquirer* newspaper. He told me how much money he was making and how fun it was. I was selling ads for Keener FM, having been made general sales manager. Gray told me of an opening at the *Enquirer* selling display ads, so I applied, got the job, and left Keener for good.

And so I entered the hell of the newspaper business.

12

A NEWSPAPERMAN?

He would sit in his office, behind glass windows,
stare at me, and yell from his office, "D'Amico,
get your ass in here!"

The job at the *Battle Creek Enquirer*, a daily newspaper in the Gannett chain, was one of the worst jobs of my life. The boss—here we go with management again—was an idiot, and I found myself hating every minute of him and the job. Yes, this just wasn't perfect for me.

When I was selling advertising for Keener FM, most advertisers said they wanted to advertise in the newspaper; when I was selling newspaper ads, they said they wanted radio. The fact is, they didn't want to spend any money at all—a fact in sales no one told me about, but that I had to learn firsthand.

I found myself sitting in a big room with a lot of desks, trying to lay out display advertising that I sold. I was lousy at that; I'm no artist. I hated it so much that I didn't want to sell anything.

My boss would sit in his office, behind glass windows, stare at me, and yell from his office, "D'Amico, get your ass in here!" He would ask why I wasn't out there selling. At 5:00 p.m., he would stand at the door and ask why I was leaving so early and why I didn't sell more.

Mistakes were not tolerated in the advertising department, and when there was one, you got docked for it, and everyone snickered. I remember one of my clients, Ying's Chinese Restaurant, whose logo appeared in an advertisement upside down. My boss was screaming; he said, "D'Amico, get your ass in here!" I was getting used to that.

I had the responsibility of tracking down who had made the mistake. It took me an entire afternoon. Art department? No. The layout department? No. Upstairs to composing, where I found the guy. I said, "Hey, do you know how this got in the paper upside down?"

He was a tough, blue-collar, union, printer type of guy. "What the hell is the problem? They're Chinese; who will notice?" Thoughts of Albany, Georgia, rushed into my mind.

The whole thing there was just horrible. I dreaded going into work. Sunday nights were especially terrible, because I couldn't stand the thought of getting up on Monday morning to drag myself in there. If there was any one job in my career that wasn't perfect for me, *this* was it! I hated every second of it.

I left after four months—but it's how I came to leave that was truly another miracle in my life and career. The next thing I knew, I was doing this really cool TV show.

13

I'M ON TV! GOT MY OWN SHOW!

I was sitting at my desk at the newspaper office. The boss was staring at me through the glass window. I was miserable, and I prayed, "Lord, please have Chuck Alvey from WUHQ-TV call and offer me a job!"

I had been on TV before. Remember my first job in Ashtabula? It seems I had a knack for it, but I didn't think much of it. I always thought TV was for blowhards, show-offs, and gasbags—"self-absorbed narcissists." Come on! You sit at a desk and read somebody else's words, and you think you're special? *Stupid business*, I thought.

But it seemed the TV news business was always calling me, or someone up there who likes me was directing me to get into television and I always resisted.

Back when I was programming Keener 14 Radio in Battle Creek, I always thought that while the power of broadcasting could be used to make money for the company, it should also be used to serve the needs of the public. It was good for me to see the station get involved in charitable organizations. It made me feel good to raise money for such organizations as the American Cancer Society, American Lung Association, ALSAC (Saint

Jude's Hospital), and other public-service endeavors. And it was good pro-gramming to have the radio personalities get involved in these efforts. We cared, and the audience knew it.

One such organization was the March of Dimes. Its people came to me and asked if our station would get involved in an annual telethon called *The March of Dimes Jail and Bail Telethon*. Prominent townspeople would be locked up in a "jail cell" on TV, and their friends and associates would phone in money to bail them out. Our DJs would be the judges, and some would be inmates, and it was fun.

After a year's experiment on a cable channel, the telethon moved to the local—and only—TV station in Battle Creek, WUHQ-TV, an ABC affiliate.

WUHQ was a very small station with no news department to speak of and hardly any local programming, with the exception of two newscasts, 6:00 and 11:00 p.m. The anchors did most of the work and all the report-ing as well. The entire news department consisted of about five or six people.

But what the station did have was a program director with a big heart and loads of vision. His name was Chuck Alvey. Chuck was one of the few TV-station-management executives whom I've worked with in my entire career who knew talent. He got it. He loved the art of television; he loved the aspect of putting on a show. He was just full of life, and he made TV what it was supposed to be—interesting and fun.

After the *Jail and Bail Telethon*, the following Monday he called me and asked if I would be interested in anchoring their newscasts. Was it a miracle? I agreed, as long as it didn't interfere with my regular radio job at Keener. He agreed to these conditions, and I accepted the job. It lasted a few months, and then the management decided to do away with news. Previous to this announcement, they had already replaced their 11:00 p.m. news with *Green Acres*. I went on with my radio career at Keener 14.

Now, at least two years had passed, I was suffering in this newspaper job, and I was at my wit's end trying to figure out how to get out and move on to something I was suited for and liked.

I hadn't talked to Chuck Alvey in some time, at least a couple years, and every day I thought about him and his TV station. I began praying to God every day and almost every hour while I was on that lousy newspaper job, affirming in my mind that God would work a miracle, that he would have Chuck Alvey call me and ask me to come back to the TV station to do something—what, I didn't know, because at the time the TV station had no local programming at all.

Now, this is hard to believe. I've told this story a number of times and most people look at me like I'm crazy, but this really happened.

I was sitting at my desk at the newspaper office. The boss was staring at me through the glass window. I was miserable, and I prayed, "Lord, please have Chuck Alvey from WUHQ-TV call and offer me a job!" And guess what.

Out of the blue, The phone at my desk rang. "Rick D'Amico speaking."

"Rick? It's Chuck Alvey. Are you happy there?"

"Hell no!"

"I got a job for you here on the *T* and *V*!" he said. (He always referred to *TV* as the *T* and *V*.) "How would you like to be our director of special events-news?" he asked.

"Oh my God, yes!" That was one of the happiest days of my life. Thank you, Lord, thank you!

I had no idea what the title of "director of special events-news" meant. All I knew was I had to do it and get out of the hellhole of selling ads for a newspaper.

I was so happy to give my notice. "I'm going back to TV!" I told that boss at the newspaper. No more "D'Amico, get your ass in here!" for me.

WUHQ-TV was a small operation, but it was a fun job as long as Alvey was there. My entire news operation consisted of the receptionist, Bev Mikalonis, and me.

They actually built a studio for me to do the evening news. It was a rip-and-read five-minute newscast every evening at 5:00 p.m. But Alvey was a visionary; he had an idea of a weekly, half-hour newsmagazine show called *On Location*.

On Location was a show before its time. Bev Mikalonis and I would travel to small towns in and around south-central Michigan and do a show. It was really good.

Individually, we would go into the town and tape a segment on its history; it seems they were all originally founded by the Potawanami Indians. We would do segments on a coffee shop or the big restaurant; on a festival the town would be having; on jobs, where I would try out a job, and we would list the job openings that week; or maybe on fitness and fun things to do for the family.

Then Bev and I would go back together and shoot the intros and wrap-arounds and close the show. The show was tightly edited and aired on Saturday night, following Leonard Nimoy's *In Search Of.* During the closing credits of that show, Nimoy would say, "Stay tuned for *On Location* with Rick D'Amico and Bev Mikalonis!" which he recorded just for us and which was played only for our audience, but that was a big thrill. The show was a success, and I loved doing it.

Another highlight of working there was the *Jerry Lewis Muscular Dystrophy Telethon.* Every year we would go to Las Vegas and attend the local host seminars. This included a three- or four-day stay at the Sahara Hotel and then, on the last day, something very special. Each local host got to shoot a local promo with Jerry Lewis.

Now, I love Jerry Lewis. I can't begin to tell you the joy I would have as a child when I watched him and Dean Martin perform on TV and in the movies. To do a shoot with Jerry Lewis was out of this world for me.

I was very nervous sitting down next to him; he could tell I was a little shaky. So he grabbed my leg, started to rub it, and yelled, "Lady, lady, Rick D'Amico, a wop from Michigan, is here. I married a wop from Michigan, and D'Amico is better looking!" We all laughed. By the way, "wop" is what Jerry Lewis called Frank Sinatra; Sinatra addressed him as "Jew." So I was impressed—if it was good enough for Frank, it was fine with me! He then whispered in my ear, "You're nervous–that's good; every time you're nervous about performing, you'll be good. That's where creativity comes from!" He was just amazing. I will never forget his words.

One day, Alvey came to me with a segment idea. It was getting close to the holidays, and he got the bright idea to demonstrate why you should not drink and drive. So he asked me to get drunk on the air! We would tape it and air it later.

I met a bunch of Michigan State Police Troopers at a huge parking lot, where they set up traffic cones. I drove the course sober and did a great job.

And then, on camera, I drank a half, maybe three-fourths, of a pint of Southern Comfort! I don't know what I blew, but the breathalyzer needle went way off the scale!

So there was a camera guy shooting in the car, with a state trooper sitting shotgun, and I was driving, drunker than snot, and guess what? I did great! I didn't knock over one cone!

"Try it again." The trooper was getting irritated. So I did, no problem; I did it fine. And again I drove the course, and still I was great! So the last time, I intentionally hit a cone to get it over with!

But I really don't remember anything after that. When I woke up later that evening, in my bed, Ruth asked, "Why were there slices of bread and bologna and watermelon all over the house?" I guess I'd been hungry when I got home and had lunch with the dog, who left part of our feast all over the kitchen and living room.

The driving-drunk piece was on tape and scheduled to run on New Year's Eve. Ruth said, "I'm inviting everyone I know over the house, and I'm going to turn the TV off!"

WUHQ-TV at this time was owned by a man who owned a letter company in Kalamazoo, Michigan. It either manufactured letters or printed them, I'm not sure.

The first general manager was a man named Hal, a great guy who walked around the station all day with a coffee cup in his hand. I'm not sure what was in the cup, but his face was always red and he slurred his words a lot. I also remember that he had a lot of company cars. After about a month, the car would have some kind of damage and would have to be replaced.

We also did a program called *Ask the Manager*. It was a live broadcast in which viewers would call in and ask the boss questions. I remember once he staggered into the studio, wobbling around; then he sat down, looked at me, and slurred, "Hey, Ron, what's happ-en-en-ing?"

I was scared to death. *This is going to be really rough!* I thought. Then the floor director said, "Stand by," and we were on.

I opened the show: "Good evening, everyone, and welcome to *Ask the Manager*. I'm Rick D'Amico with our vice president and general manager. How are you doing this evening?" He looked into the camera and without missing a beat, spoke eloquently and perfectly. I was amazed.

Hal departed the station to "pursue other interests," as they always say, and the next general manager was the chief engineer, Lee Stevens. Stevens was an idiot. Management! He knew nothing about TV, and he hated Alvey. Alvey was the lifeblood of the station, who knew programming and was well liked. Not long after, Alvey moved on to WNEM-TV in Saginaw, Michigan. My show was doomed; I was doomed.

Alvey offered me a job as the main anchor of their evening newscasts at WNEM-TV in Saginaw, Michigan, an NBC affiliate. Ruth and I drove up to Saginaw to take a look, and we thought it was the pits—about as ugly as Flint. I turned it down. I just couldn't see raising a family there.

Lee Stevens never quite made the switch from dressing as a chief engineer to dressing as a general manager. His wife, as rumor had it, dressed him. He wore orange shirts with purple ties and green suits! It's as though his wife was an interior designer in a cathouse.

Stevens, being a chief engineer, really didn't have a handle on running a TV station, and especially a sales department. I remember the sales manager always running through the station screaming, "What kind of hamburger operation is this?" That became another one of my trademark expressions throughout my career.

And an incident I'll never forget: A salesman ran into my office one day and asked if I could cover the opening of a K-Mart. I said, "I don't think we could do that."

"And why not?" he asked.

"Well, for one thing, our newscast is only five minutes, and we can't waste time on the opening of a K-Mart."

"You don't have to *run* the story," he said. "Just show up with an empty camera and make it look like you're shooting it, and I'll tell the client the story didn't make the final cut to be on our evening news." Could you believe a TV station would do that?

Probably because he hated Alvey and my show was Alvey's idea and production, Stevens canceled my show *On Location*, and I had nothing to do. I would sit in my office all day and read newspapers, and then I would do the five-minute live newscast at 5:00 p.m. and go home. I was bored to death. This was not perfect for me! I made an appointment with Stevens and asked what my future was at the station. All I remember was Stevens telling me that the future of news on TV was doomed; he said TV stations could no longer afford to do news, and news on television would soon die. This was 1978. Now *here* was a television-station vice president and general manager with real insight, a visionary! Management!

What I told him next was a shining moment in my career. "I have nothing to do here; I'm bored. I'm going to go home, and you give me a call when you decide what my future here is," I said. I walked out of his office and stayed home for a couple of months, and they still paid me.

In the meantime, I lined up a job at WBCK Radio in Battle Creek doing the morning show. I was working at WBCK and still getting paid by the TV station. Most mornings I would make fun of WUHQ-TV and, of course, management.

Finally, the WUHQ program director called me and asked me to turn in my key, which I did, and I got a final check.

And now I was back in radio and stuck with another management type who knew nothing about talent.

14

WBCK IN BATTLE CREEK

"You can just take this job and shove it."

WBCK was what I like to call an "old line"—an old-fashioned, middle-of-the-road-type radio station, with older personalities and pop standard music.

It had just been sold, and the new owner was the former general manager of WWJ in Detroit. His name was Nat, and he was irritating just like a gnat! A sharp dresser, he thought he was a big-city businessman who had come to the small town, with his big-city ways, to light up the place. He ran the station, and he liked me because I had worked on TV and he thought I would be a good addition to the established morning team of Dave Eddy and Tom McHale.

Dave Eddy was an institution in Battle Creek radio; he had been doing the morning show for years. He was a smooth-talking personality who was just right for a morning audience. He was practically a household word in south-central Michigan. And, I must say, he was a really nice guy too. He was just wonderful, and by the way, the only non-Keener person to attend our Keener Reunion thirty years later.

The only problem was, when I joined him on the morning show, he had just gone into business with a local TV store and was cutting back his hours at the station. He would leave at about 8:30 a.m. to be at the TV store for its opening at 9:00 a.m. Then the gnat would come in at nine thirty and yell at me for our morning antics.

Dave and I had so much fun together, laughing and giggling through the whole show, making fun and having fun. Then Dave would leave. The gnat, the general manager, would walk into the studio at around nine thirty, put his hand on my shoulder, and say something like, "You guys are not doing it right; you're goofing around too much. When you're off the air, come into my office; we have to retool the whole show."

Johnny Carson was a huge personality at the time, and one of his favorite expressions was "I didn't know that." I would say that often after Dave Eddie would come with some ad-lib that led us into something funny. The gnat would criticize me for saying this: "You can't say that; it sounds like you're stupid." Well, if *Johnny Carson* was stupid, *I* wanted to be stupid! This manager was a piece of work.

This was not perfect for me—especially because I was a guy who had not had a good track record dealing with management. And to make things even worse, I had just gotten into the Amway business, and I thought I was on the verge of becoming a millionaire. The entire Amway thing was one of the biggest disasters of my life, and it deserves its own chapter.

The gnat, as I mentioned, was the former general manager of WWJ in Detroit. Every morning for a thousand years, WWJ was spanked, demolished, in the ratings by WJR and by one of the most talented morning-radio personalities of all time, anywhere: JP McCarthy. So at his Battle Creek Station, the gnat wanted me to be JP McCarthy. I'm not JP McCarthy; I'm Rick D'Amico!

After two or three sessions with Gnat the manager telling me how rotten I was on the air and how things had to change to his liking, I—and here's another shining moment in my broadcasting career—told him, "I'm sick and tired of you telling me how bad I am. Everything with you is negative, nothing positive. You can just take this job and shove it up your ass!" And I stormed out of his office, got my jacket, ran out the back door, jumped into my Cadillac Coup Deville, and sped off. (I had to have the Cadillac for my Amway career!)

And as I was speeding down the drive, he ran out the front door and threw himself in front of my car, waving his hands. I slammed on the brakes and almost ran him over. I lowered the passenger-side window. He looked in and said, "You think you're some big-time son-of-a-bitch Amway guy making tons of money, a big shot."

I just smiled; I was in my glory.

He then said, and here's another shocker, "Come back tomorrow, do the show, and afterward we will make things right."

But he and I just didn't get along, and not long after that, I was so disgusted with him and so fed up I did something I've always wanted to do in my radio career. One morning the alarm went off. I dreaded going into work and facing that jerk of a boss who constantly criticized me, so I hit the snooze button a couple of times, rolled over, and said, "I'm done!" I flipped on the radio and listened. No one was there. Why? Because I hadn't shown up! I turned off the radio and went back to sleep, something most every morning-show person wants to do at least once in his or her career. This was the end of my job at WBCK.

On August 9, 2009, about thirty years later, I found myself in the studios of WBCK in Battle Creek, in town for the Keener Radio Reunion, and I was on the air with former Keener DJs Roy Lafountain, Bill Gray, and Dave Hoppe. We were reminiscing, and I apologized to the audience for not showing up that morning.

But, hey, I was going to be rich—in Amway. That's next!

15

AMWAY: I'M GOING TO BE RICH!

No one got in the business; they just kept bowing their heads and laughing as they walked out the door!

After WBCK, Ruth and I tried to make a go of it in the Amway business. It didn't work out.

Amway is a wonderful worldwide company headquartered in Ada, Michigan. There are people in the Amway business who are very successful and make tons of money, but it was not to be for Ruth and me.

Amway is a business of direct sales. You make money by selling products (good products, I might add) and sponsoring people to be in business with you. You make the big money from the overall volume your business organization does. The more products you buy wholesale from the Amway Corporation for your entire organization to resell, the more bonuses you make, and when one of your sponsored salespeople reaches a certain sales volume, he or she breaks away from you, and you earn overrides, or residuals, from that person's business. It's like owning a bunch of McDonald's restaurants around the world, where you're getting a piece of the action of every store. So the real money is in sponsoring as many people as you can to sell and to get *them* to sponsor as many people as *they* can. I know it sounds like a pyramid scheme, but it's not.

Ruth and I were living in a beautiful home on a wonderfully wooded street in Battle Creek, Michigan. My neighbor, a police officer, invited us over for a get-together. It was a Saturday afternoon.

When Ruth and I got there, a bunch of people were sitting around, most of them police officers, and we were wondering what the heck this was all about.

A man in a three-piece suit was standing in front of a whiteboard on an easel. "Hello," he began, "I'm Sergeant Steve DiMattio from the Battle Creek Police Department, and I want to show you something." I thought this was some type of recruitment for the Neighborhood Watch. He went through this whole presentation, drawing circles and talking about moving products into a system and making hundreds of thousands of dollars a year. He never mentioned what this business was or the name of the company. He finished, looked at the whiteboard, and said, "Isn't this wonderful?"

I raised my hand. "What is the name of the company?"

He said, "Amway!"

Someone in the back of the room screamed, "Oh shit, it's a trap!"

I, honestly, had never heard of Amway, so why was this guy trying to hide the name of the company?

That's the way the Amway business was presented to us: don't tell anyone what it is when you invite them to a presentation. Tell them you don't have to sell anything; all you have to do is get people to sign up.

At the time, I was leaving WUHQ-TV and on the air on WBCK Radio, and with my reputation and popularity in the small town of Battle Creek, I thought I probably could do well. I got in and found myself working the Amway business with my partners, a bunch of street cops. There were times, in the middle of business meetings when we were to present our business to prospective distributors, that my partners would scatter out of the room, with walkie-talkies blazing, leaving me there all by myself to make the presentation. Could you imagine what was going through the people's minds?

Sergeant DiMattio and his wife, Mary Ann, were in charge, our "up-line," as they call it in direct marketing, and were tough cookies. My other partner was Neil Vanderbilt a great guy; he and I were best friends, and his wife, Elaine, and Ruth were best friends.

We rented an office and hired a telephone-answering service. Here's how it worked. I would run an ad in the paper that said something like, "Advertising, public relations, marketing, and distribution person needed. Call Rick D'Amico." People would call the answering service. The operator would say I was out and would call them back. Then I called them back and told them to meet me at the office of my business, "Intermark." (Intermark was short for "international marketing.") DiMattio and Vanderbuilt also made appointments for people to show up at the office for the same presentation, and all our distributors did the same.

The evening of the meeting, there might be forty or fifty people packed into the room, all wondering what this was about. I would stand before them, introduce myself, and do the presentation. At the end, I would say, "Isn't this wonderful?"

Someone would ask, "What's the name of the company?"

I would say, "Amway!"

Someone would say, "Oh shit—no!" And then everyone would walk out. After the room cleared, there would be perhaps one or two little old ladies sitting in the back of the room smiling. We would recruit them and never see them again.

Ruth and I did, however, through talking with hundreds of people, including many of our friends and family members, end up with a whole bunch of believers and distributors all around the world, including in Japan and Germany.

I remember doing a presentation for one of my distributors, whose wife was from Japan. She was working for a Japanese company located in Battle Creek, and she invited her coworkers to the meeting. Everything I said had to be translated into Japanese. My English words in their language sounded so funny that I began to laugh every time the translator spoke. I was telling them how they would become wealthy, and the translator said, "Yｕ fukuna!" *Yu fuk una?* I thought. *They're telling me to you know what!*

When it was all over, everyone was laughing. I don't know if those people were laughing at me or with me, but I do know this: No one got in the business. They just kept bowing their heads and laughing as they walked out the door.

One of my distributors ran into Betsy Palmer at Cleveland Hopkins Airport. (Palmer was one of the original female hosts on the *Today* show on NBC, a star on national quiz shows like *What's My Line*, and an actress. She starred in some of the *Friday the 13th* movies.) Anyway, she invited us over to her farmhouse in Kalamazoo to tell her about the business. She got in! We invited her to a big Amway rally at the Amway world headquarters in Ada, Michigan. I introduced her, and the crowd went wild. Afterward, she went back to New York, and we never heard from her again.

One of our best distributors and a good friend, an African American, had people in Detroit and wanted me to go with him to do a meeting in the Motor City.

We were driving through a bombed-out neighborhood, as a lot of Detroit remains today. And he said, "Now, listen, when we get there, after parking the car, we have to run in the house real fast. If we don't, we might get shot."

The meeting was horrible; people kept coming and going throughout the entire presentation. Later, I was told some people there were packing heat. Armed! I don't disparage anyone from carrying a firearm for self-protection, but it made nervous anyway.

Afterward, when we were driving home in my white Cadillac Coupe Deville, a cop car with lights flashing pulled us over. Two cops got out of the car; one said, "Driver's license, registration, and proof of insurance."

I said, "What's the problem, Officer?"

"You didn't come to a complete stop at the intersection. The definition of 'stop' is when your wheels come to a complete stop for at least one second." Then he took a good look at me and said, "Hey, you're Rick D'Amico!" He let us go. But I wondered if the reason he stopped us was because it was a white Cadillac and my friend in the car was black.

Most of the distributors in Amway were couples, husband and wives usually. By the time it was all over, many got divorced, including Sgt. Steve DiMattio and his wife, Mary Ann.

Mention Amway to Ruth to this day, and she will say, "Divorce!" It's kind of funny.

As you can surmise, this is not the way to run a business. Amway is a great company and deserves to be mentioned as a company to be proud of, and its name should be brought out up front. Also, if you tell people they don't have to sell anything, they won't sell anything. Money is made by buying products from the Amway Corporation, and the products have to be sold at a retail level, at a profit, or else somebody gets stuck with a bunch of products in his or her basement.

When it was over, Ruth and I were the ones stuck with a bunch of products in our basement, to the tune of $6,000. We got out. I had no job.

16

NO ONE WANTS YOU WHEN YOU'RE DOWN AND OUT

"Where are you working now?"
"I'm not working now."

Trying to find a job when you don't have one is almost impossible. This was a rough time in my career. I sent out hundreds of résumés and audition tapes and got very few replies. For every twenty tapes I sent out, I probably got one "no thanks." Today, no one at all would answer this type of request.

If I were fortunate enough to get to talk to someone, the employer would ask, "Where are you working now?"

How do you answer that? "I'm not working now." That's death. No one wants to hire someone out of work.

I should mention here that Ruth was working and supporting the family. She was the executive secretary to the chairman of the board and president of the Battle Creek Equipment Company, a small health- and exercise-equipment manufacturer. She had always made more money than I did. Radio never paid that well.

I had burned my bridges at WBCK, and WUHQ-TV, Keener Radio, was automated, although I did pick up some part-time gigs there. But it was no fun anymore, and I spent a lot of time on the phone talking to friends in the business trying to find anything. It was like starting all over again.

A friend told me about a DJ shift at WKMI in Kalamazoo, Michigan; I applied and got it. WKMI was a good station with a good reputation in Michigan as being a professionally run Top 40 rocker. It was overnight, weekends, and only part-time. But here's the upside: I was working! When I applied for a job after that and the would-be boss asked, "Where are you working now?" I could answer, "WKMI in Kalamazoo!"

Also, no one, it seems, likes to hire strangers. Remember my experiences in the past—it's friends of friends who talk you up and who make recommendations that get you in the door. And that's what happened next.

Back in my days at Keener Radio, Kevin Sanderson, the high-school student who came to the station to pick up our music surveys and hung around almost every day until I hired him, had moved on to Detroit. At his station there, he worked with a weekend part-time DJ who was full-time at WILS Radio in Lansing, Michigan. She told him of a program-director opening there; he told her about me, and she told her Lansing boss about me. I was in!

17

WORKING FOR A RED BIRD

*I had no idea at the time, but this was paving
the way for my permanent career in television.*

Following the career of a radio DJ is like following the career of a ro-
deo cowboy. So many towns, so many gigs: as George Strait puts it in
"Amarillo by Morning," "They took my saddle in Houston / Broke my leg
in Santa Fe…"

In 1981, a man whose last name was Byrd owned WILS-AM and FM
in Lansing, Michigan. His nickname was Red, probably because of the
hair he used to have. So yes, he was called "Red Byrd." He was probably
the nicest man I've ever met in the radio business.

Mr. Byrd was in a wheelchair; he had arthritis really badly. His daughter, Susan, was the station manager, and she ran the station. I loved her; in
fact, the entire Byrd family was wonderful to me, and I really enjoyed my
time with them.

WILS-AM was one of those legendary Top 40 stations that had domi-
nated the Lansing, Michigan, audience in the sixties and seventies. By
time I got there, though, it was in a shambles. No one listened. There were
many reasons why; the primary reason was that FM had taken hold in the

market, and Lansing had become one of the top cities in the United States for FM listenership. So I had my work cut out for me on an AM station.

WILS-FM was a monster, album-oriented, blue-collar, rock station that was killing everybody. So my job was just to make the AM viable. What a challenge!

My plan was to change the music format to rock-and-roll oldies, and I would institute a marketing campaign called "Time to Come on Home," which we used to tell potential listeners, "Come on home to where it all began, to your friends. Come home to 1320 WILS." I had a two-and-a-half-minute song produced with that theme, and we played it in a rotation as if it were a hit record. I also had jingles produced from that song to introduce records and ID the station.

I got all the DJs together and told them they were all going to be personalities, and they loved that. We also had the best news department in town, with the best newscasters. And we were a CBS affiliate, meaning we carried ten minutes of CBS news on the hour and local news on the half hour and had reporters at the statehouse and on the street.

Keith Cummings, our news director, was amazing. He sounded like a major-market, network newscaster. Keith also did Michigan State football and basketball play-by-play.

One DJ who was really instrumental in making our station a success was Gail McKnight. She was the one who worked part-time in Detroit and who, upon Kevin Sanderson's recommendation, got me hired at WILS. I made Gail our music director, meaning she was second in command and in charge of every record that would be played. We would spend long hours going over every record in the library, only picking the major oldie hits. We worked twelve- to fourteen-hour, sometimes even eighteen-hour, days just to get the format started.

We also spent an agonizing time going over the format—which records to be played at certain times, news intros, everything. She was incredible.

Susan Harvey, the station manager, gave me free rein and control. After a few months, she told me, "If you do nothing else at this station for the rest of your life, what you've done up till now makes you the best program director we've ever had."

In addition to running the station, I also did the morning show. I instituted such features as On This Day in History, Thought of the Day, and News of the Weird, which I also did years later on Channel 10 in Phoenix.

I got a comedian to do impersonations. He would call in as Richard Nixon and Henry Kissinger regularly. I also did a funny bit called "Michigan Outdoors with Ted Nugent." We had the comedian imitating Nugent hunting deer with bazookas, tanks, and hand grenades. We got a lot of calls on that.

Every morning at 7:29 a.m., I did "March around the Breakfast Table," which I stole from the old ABC Radio show *Don McNeil's Breakfast Club*. I usually played the Michigan State fight song, by the Michigan State marching band. That was big.

I wasn't working with a big budget, and we had no on-air meteorologist, so every morning, before I went on the air, I called Ruth at home and read her the weather forecast, which she wrote down along with an insulting one-liner. So when it came time for the weather, I had "the Weather Lady" with the weather. It went something like this: "It's ten minutes after six on 1320 WILS. It's time for the weather; here's the Weather Lady!"

"Thank you, Rick. It's going to be a great day today, cloudy with a high of forty-four degrees, colder tonight, with an overnight low of twenty-five degrees. Tomorrow it will be warmer, with a high of fifty. Oh, by the way…Rick, do you ever wonder what life would be like if you'd had enough oxygen at birth?" No one knew she was my wife; everyone loved her, and by the way, she hated to do this.

I also had my daughter on the phone, as "the Child Star," with some funny show-business news. She would say something like: "In Hollywood, the latest craze is the Mickey Rooney cocktail; you have one drink, and you're under the table!"

I used the copywriter, a good friend, Sandy Robbins, to be "the Word Lady" with the word of the day. All this was just ridiculous, fun shtick, as I call it, and was hilarious.

The ratings were going up. I was happy.

I also hired one of the funniest radio personalities I had ever heard, Charlie Fredrick. If you walked into the studio while he was on the air, he would put you on the show, carry on a conversation with you, and turn it into a comedy routine. Almost every day he had stories about his cat, Felix, and everyone loved Charlie; he was a good friend.

Another DJ I remember was Dan Coyle. When looking over his résumé, I was shocked to read he was a nuclear physicist at Michigan State University. He just wanted to play the hits part-time on our station.

I was always looking for opportunities to get our station as much publicity as possible. As in Battle Creek, I got our station involved in the local telethons, such as those for the Children's Miracle Network and Easter Seals. I appeared on camera along with the other WILS DJs, raising money, reading pledges, and generally hosting an hour or two. I had no idea at the time, but this was paving the way for my permanent career in television.

About this time, our second daughter, Jessica Marie, was born. I was sweating this one out. She was due to arrive in December, and I was worried there would be one of those vicious Michigan snowstorms or ice storms and we would be stranded in our apartment. Ruth was getting a little tired of us doing dry runs driving to the hospital. Turns out, it was a cold New Year's Eve night when Jessica was born, with no snow, and we made it to Sparrow Hospital in no time. Oh, and there's no truth to the rumor that I had Ruth jumping up and down on the stairs to make sure the baby was born on New Year's Eve, so I could get that tax exemption!

I remember bringing Jessica home from the hospital; she seemed to be so bright and so curious. She was lying in her bassinet and staring up at the pictures we had on the wall. As it turned out, her curiosity stayed with her in her adult years, because she's now working as the head copywriter for a major online retailer and still keeping her hands in journalism, writing for a broadcast wire service and network in her spare time.

WILS turned out to be a good station, with strong news and public service, great personalities, and rocking oldies. But still, getting an audience on an AM station was really tough. The ratings were way up, but always mediocre.

So when a fast-talking, young, and seemingly too sincere new radio-station owner came along and offered me ownership in his station, I jumped at the chance. What a mistake!

18

A HAUNTED RADIO STATION

*The man had been murdered, and get this,
he was wearing a plaid jacket.*

Chuck was a young attorney and CPA who had this innocent look about him. He oozed sincerity and honesty, and when talking to you, he'd raise his eyebrows with the look of a young child who'd never told a lie.

He was the new owner of a small AM and FM radio station in Saint Johns, Michigan, a few miles north of Lansing, which he wanted to make a big-time Lansing country-music-radio powerhouse. He'd even had the FM tower raised to a higher elevation so the station could be heard in the Lansing metro area. He hired me to run the station. I was to be the general manager, general sales manager, part of the morning on-air team, and his partner as part owner. He laid out the terms of my contract on a yellow legal pad, which he carried wherever he went. And when the final papers were drawn up, after I had resigned from WILS and started working for him, after we shook hands and looked each other in the eye and agreed to the deal, he changed all the terms—the bonus structure cut drastically and ownership percentage cut. Also, part of the deal was to provide a company car, and it took almost a year for him to deliver on this. Management! *Already* this was not perfect for me.

However, there were some highlights from working at the new K-92 Continuous Country.

One of my duties was to train the young sales staff, so I immediately went to the library and got a sales-training book by Tom Hopkins. He is a leading, internationally known sales trainer. More than thirty years later, while I was working the morning TV show in Phoenix, he sent me a letter; he had watched our show and was a big fan. I wrote back telling him how important he was to our sales training at K-92.

Also, I enlisted every salesperson in the Dale Carnegie Sales Course. It was a grueling course, consisting of a lot of classroom lectures and home-work, and it was competitive. All the students had to compete with one another, and at the end, a "sales talk champion" would be named. And guess who was named sales talk champion? Yeah, me! To this day, I'm very proud of that accomplishment.

The K-92 studios were in a haunted shack on a country road, in a for-est, between Saint Johns and Lansing—*haunted* meaning it was haunted by a ghost! Really! More on that later.

Our young owner wanted to relocate the station's main offices to downtown Lansing. So I put on my best three-piece suit and visited some of the nicest, most professional office buildings downtown, in view of the state capitol dome. I was thinking, *This is really cool—I'm part owner of a radio station with offices in a downtown high-rise. I've finally made it!*

Well, not so fast. One of the station's investors was a guy who owned the Total Gas Stations in Lansing. So when it came time to relocate the station's main offices to Lansing, he offered an office suite for free. Guess where it was located. Yep, you knew this was coming—in a gas station! Now, when I say "gas station," I'm not saying a former gas station, or a former gas station that was remodeled into a business office. Nope. A gas station, a real, working gas station!

Facing the gas station, on the right, was the store, where you paid for the gas and bought MoonPies. On the left, what was once a garage had been sealed off and made into offices. And that's where we ran K-92. People would wander in to pay for gas, complain that the air hose didn't work, or ask for directions; it was horrible.

One day, one of my big advertising-agency clients insisted on coming to the station to drop off his copy, and I tried to talk him out of it, but he insisted. I gave him the directions, telling him it was the Total Gas Station and to be sure and walk in the door on the left.

He walked in the door on the right, completely dumbfounded. "Is there a radio station here?" he asked.

"Walk out the door you came in and then walk in the next door to the garage," the clerk answered.

He walked into my office and was completely astounded. "When you said gas station, you *meant* gas station!"

The entire experience at this place was surreal. When bills came in the mail, Charles would throw them away without even opening them. He used to say, "If you don't open them, you don't have to pay them."

The big day came when we were about to premiere the new station. We had a big media bash, a cocktail reception at one of the downtown hotels, and invited advertising agencies and city dignitaries. Our country-radio consultants flew in from Dallas, and generally the who's who in town were there.

Chuck, the owner, perhaps was drinking a little too much. I got up onstage and spoke to the crowd, welcoming them, and selling our new type of country radio. And then I introduced the boss. "And now, ladies and gentlemen, I would like to introduce to you the man who is the owner and spirit behind K-92...blah, blah..."

Charles took the mike and said, "Yeah, well, I got my dick in the wringer for a couple hundred thousand dollars, so this better work or I'm screwed!" The crowd was stunned.

We had a great air staff. I stole Charlie Fredrick from WILS; he was, as I said in the last chapter, one of the funniest men I've ever met. I sat in with Fredrick on the morning show for a couple of hours, then drove down to the gas station in Lansing to run the station. We hit our nut within three months (expenses), and I believe after that the station was profitable under ol' Charles's accounting procedures.

The studios, still in that shack in the woods north of Lansing, hold the distinction of being the crappiest I have ever worked in. One morning, the news director forgot his key, so he banged the door down completely off the hinges. Charles did not replace the door for weeks, and all kinds of bugs—you know, the kind that live in a Michigan forest—infested the station. Meanwhile, the toilets were so dirty you couldn't tell if they needed to be flushed!

But the real story of K-92 was the ghost. The DJs were always complaining about strange things happening to them. Our evening female personality complained of seeing a man in a plaid jacket standing in the window or wandering through the station, but when she went to see him, he was gone. One evening, a block calendar flew off the desk and hit her. At times when leaving the station, she saw a light in the woods that seemed to follow her.

Some of the DJs said that while they were talking on the air, they'd see someone wearing a plaid jacket in their peripheral vision, standing beside them; they would look over, and the vision would be gone. Tapes would stop for no reason. Equipment turned itself on and then off and then on again.

One of the toughest and most hardened DJs on the staff was a factory worker who came in part-time because he loved country music. He was a tough, hardworking, blue-collar type of guy, and I respected him. I pulled him aside one day and said, "What's going on here? You don't think there's a ghost, do you?"

And he replied, "Rick, I've seen a lot of shit in my life, and I'll tell you, that studio is haunted!"

And here's how I became a believer. One day, I was filling in for the afternoon jock. I was all alone in the station. A music sweep was playing; all our music was on reel-to-reel tape players. Out of the blue, the tape recorder playing the song on the air stopped. I ran into the main studio and hit the play button. *How'd that happen?* I thought.

I was alone in the studio, and it was time for the evening DJ to come in and take over. I was in the production studio, reading into the mike, and saw, through my peripheral vision, someone walk by me. I, of course, knew it had to be the evening DJ walking into the main studio. I finished my work and walked into the studio to say hello, and no one was there. I walked through the station looking for someone, anyone—but no one was there; I was all alone!

Finally someone got the idea to hire some psychics, or ghost busters, if you will, to come into the studio and find out once and for all if we had a ghost. But, being the skeptic I am, I also did something secretly. I asked the news director to go down to the county courthouse and look up the records of the property to find out anything unusual that might have happened there and to not say a word to anyone.

The psychics came in and chanted. They said things, walked around, and talked to the spirit. Their report was that a man who was wronged by a woman had died on the property and refused to leave. They said they walked him out of the studio and sent him on his way to the "other side."

And what about the news director's report from the county courthouse? He found records indicating that a man's body had been found on the property many years ago, wrapped in barbed wire, lying in a ditch. The man had been murdered, and get this, he had been wearing a plaid jacket!

A year or two later, I was teaching a course in radio broadcasting at Lansing Community College, and I was getting a cup of coffee before class. One of the professors said to me, "Hey, Rick, how was your time at K-92? When I worked at the station many years ago, we always thought the station was haunted."

"Yeah, me too!" I said, grinning.

19

WHY LANSING, MICHIGAN, HATED ME

The city was in shock. The* Lansing State Journal *wrote terrible things about us. And who was the face of all this to the public? Me!

The whole thing at K-92 was surreal, and as you can imagine, not perfect for me.

My old station, WILS, had been sold to a big insurance company. It was bringing in a big-shot, corporate vice president to be the general manager, and the rumor was he wanted me to run it.

I called and asked for an interview. We set up a lunch. I made sure I looked the part of corporate: navy-blue suit, white shirt, blue tie, and then my shoes—I looked down, and they needed to be shined. Should I shine them? Who would know? *He'll never notice, but shine them anyway*, I thought, and I did.

I met Bruce Hendrickson at a hotel restaurant. He was dressed in a business suit and looked like a first-class businessman.

I approached him, looked straight in his eyes, and said, "I'm very happy to meet you." I held his gaze to make sure he would look away first, wanting him to know I enjoyed his company. And what do you know? He looked straight down at my shoes, noticed the spit shine, and then checked out my suit. His eyes moved back to my own, and he said, "I'm happy to meet you too, Rick; let's get some lunch."

I point this out because first, he was an insurance executive and second, I did some research on him and found he was a former mayor of a small town in Wisconsin; a former member of the Wisconsin governor's cabinet; and, get this, a former candidate for Congress. His title at the insurance company was director of administrative services, which meant he could do anything he wanted until he ran for Congress again.

But his interests were in broadcasting, and his ambition was to make WILS a success and then to become the head of all the radio stations the company owned, about five, as I recall. I, as he told me in our interview, would have the opportunity to become the national program director of all the stations. This was turning out to be a big-time job interview!

However, it didn't go very well. "What college did you go to?" he asked.

"I didn't go to college."

"Well, how did you get to be where you are?"

"I've loved radio ever since I was twelve. I joined the air force when I got out of high school, got a job in radio, and have worked ever since," I responded.

He changed direction. "I love to ski, cross-country, do a lot of it in Wisconsin. Do you ski?"

"Me? No, I hate the winter, never go outside!"

"What kind of sports are you involved in?"

"None," I said.

"Play sports in high school?" he asked.

"No, I was the band announcer!" That didn't go over very well. Driving home, I thought, *Well, I blew that.*

Two days later he called and offered me the job. Here's what I found out later: He told me technical qualifications have little to do with getting hired, unless, of course, we're talking about a brain surgeon or airline pilot. Ninety-nine percent is based on whether your boss likes you. Bruce liked me because I was a hardworking, blue-collar guy who had worked my way up and was honest without trying to impress him. I'd just told the truth.

Bruce could be described as very demanding, but I learned so much from him, worked so hard for him, was so challenged by him, and found him to be such a character that I liked him very much.

He was a perfectionist; from the clothes he wore (and the clothes he expected *you* to wear) to the minutiae (I learned that word from him; he used it so much) of how the carpets were cleaned in the station, everything had to be perfect. In the creative world of radio broadcasting, that doesn't always work.

Here are some examples: The entire station appearance did not meet his high standards, so he had it remodeled to the tune of thousands of dollars. We had long meetings every morning and afternoon. He was explaining how much he was spending and said, "And thousands of dollars for signage."

"What's signage?" I asked.

He looked at me with his usual cold stare. "The signs on the walls outside the offices, the signs in front of the building, the signs to tell employees where everything is...signage." That was his orientation; everything had to be tidy, everything in place.

He would walk through the parking lot and call me outside. "Who belongs to that green beater over there?" *Beater* was his word for a junky car.

"The Ford?"

"Yeah, the Ford."

"The overnight DJ, Tony Clark."

Cold stare again. "It's a piece of shit; have it towed out of here." And he meant it—if Bruce didn't like your car, he would have it removed from the parking lot.

Our AM station carried Michigan State football, and one Saturday morning, the play-by-play team was flying to Madison, Wisconsin, to do the game. He wanted to go along and bring me with him. He invited me to go up to Stevens Point, Wisconsin, after the game to spend time at company headquarters.

It was a cold, rainy, and foggy morning in Lansing. We all got in the plane, a tiny aircraft with just one propeller. The pilot was also a member of our play-by-play team. As we taxied down the runway, just about ready to be airborne, he said, "Shit!"

Bruce said, "Something wrong?"

The pilot said, "Damn. Can't get the horizon indicator to work." He turned the plane around; we were back in the terminal. Good thing, or I wouldn't be here today.

But Bruce got on the phone; called company headquarters; and in an hour, a company Falcon jet swooped out of the sky, picked us up, and flew us to the game. But just before we boarded the aircraft, he gave his cold stare to the pilot and said, "You're not coming; you almost put our lives in jeopardy, so you stay behind." Later, while on the flight to Wisconsin, he said to me, "That son of a bitch should have checked out the plane before we got on; he almost killed us!"

WILS-AM was still a middle-of-the-road oldies station, while WILS-FM was the undisputed number-one, hard-rocking, blue-collar, heavy-metal, rock-and-roll radio station, and Hendrickson hated it. I, by the way, didn't hate it; I just didn't understand it!

All the DJs looked like refugees from a work-release program from the state prison; they had long hair, earrings, tattoos, black T-shirts decorated with skulls—you know, Ozzy Osbourne stuff. Hendrickson, a buttoned-down Ivy Leaguer, cringed when he saw them in the hallways, hated to talk to them, and couldn't stand them, their music, and everything the station stood for.

Also, Bruce didn't like the AM news director. The man just didn't hit it off with him, didn't respond correctly to his questions, and didn't look the part. He always acted as though he wasn't listening to what you were saying, with hardly any eye contact, a no-no for Hendrickson. However, on the air he was awesome. Hendrickson didn't care, and one day while having a meeting with him, he didn't like the news director's attitude, so he fired him right there on the spot.

The very next morning, about 5:30 a.m. (Bruce always got up early to do yoga), my phone rang; I was sound asleep.

"Hello," I finally answered.

"This is Bruce; are you listening to the radio?" he asked.

"No."

"Turn it on now!"

I did, and guess what. The fired news director was on the air! He didn't believe, or perhaps wasn't paying attention to, the fact that he had been fired. He went into work the day after he was fired. I had to go in, fire him, and escort him out of the station for a second time.

We hired John Lund, a radio consultant from San Francisco, and the plan was to do a research project to discover what to do to change the FM. In the first meeting with Lund, Hendrickson said, "If research shows to keep the FM as it is, we're going to change it anyway, because I hate that heavy-rock-metal stuff!" He never did catch on and say "heavy metal."

The research showed, according to Lund, that the station should change to a format to attract eighteen-to-forty-nine-year-old women. Lund said, "We'll keep the call letters WILS, play love songs, and call it LS-102."

Bruce and I, in the meantime, automated the AM, and most of the DJs were fired; some were held over to be on the FM after the big change. One of our AM DJs, Dan Drolett, was locked away in an apartment, secretly dubbing love songs to tape cartridges to be played on the new FM. Before the day came, I had to fire all the FM DJs, one by one. I had to call each one in my office, one at a time and face-to-face, and let them go; I hated every second of it.

And then it was time for the new love-songs station to premiere.

A couple of days before the new love-songs format was to go on the air, Lund was in the station, and we got together for a chat. He said, "The new ratings just came out, and guess what; the FM [with the old heavy-metal format] is far and away the number-one station in Lansing. We're making a big mistake!"

The last song played on the old station, on a Saturday morning, was Jim Morrison and the Doors, "This Is the End." The station went silent for a few hours and signed back on with Dionne Warwick's "Do You Know the Way to San Jose?" She was one of my favorites, after all; we were friends from my Ohio days, remember? My oldest daughter called (she was fifteen at the time). "Dad, it sounds like AM!"

The city was in shock. Mike Hughes, the media writer for the *Lansing State Journal,* wrote terrible things about us. And who was the face of all this to the public? Me! My picture was in the paper as the villain. I was the spokesman; I was the bad guy.

Bruce, at the time, was negotiating with Michigan State University over football play-by-play rights, and something went wrong. The *Lansing State Journal* didn't do a good job of reporting it. It was that Mike Hughes again; he hated us for what we'd done to WILS-FM, so he made it look bad.

Somebody at corporate headquarters didn't like what was going on. It was a big insurance company that wanted to maintain a low profile. So Bruce left, and my job was doomed.

I knew it the morning I saw the biggest buffoon I'd ever met in broadcasting walk into the building. He was Hendrickson's replacement. Here comes the Huggy Buffoon!

Now, before we move on, let me report to you how strange life can be. Over thirty years later—thirty years!—I get an e-mail from guess who. It was Bruce! He had moved to Phoenix; he was in town and wanted to have lunch. We met at a restaurant in Scottsdale, and what was one of the first things he did? He looked down at my shoes! "How're your shoes? You always wore shiny shoes; I'll never forget that!"

Bruce and I have become friends and have had lunch a few times, and both of us are so thankful we survived the Lansing radio wars.

20

THE HUGGY BUFFOON

*"I couldn't work there after what they said
to me!"*

Before I begin to tell you about the biggest buffoon I have ever had to
work for, let me say that some of the people I worked with at WILS were
awesome.

Dan Drolett, Dan Renton, Tony Clark, and Sandy Robbins are some
of the many people who worked their hearts out to be good broadcasters.
I'm sure I've forgotten many people, and I apologize. We worked so hard
and had so much fun, but when the buffoon arrived, things got really dark.

Lansing TV sports anchor John Matlack, whom I later shared an office with when I got back into television, and I used to laugh at the weird-
ness of the business we were in. He used to say, "You know, Rick, I can't
figure out if this business *makes* assholes or *attracts* assholes." The next boss
in my life had me write that thought in my mind indelibly for the rest of
my career.

The new general manager of WILS came walking up the sidewalk,
past the window in my office, and I was in shock. He was about six foot
four; had bleached blond hair with black roots showing; wore a white suit,

red shirt, and white tie; and had a swagger that meant trouble. I thought, *This man is a general manager? He looks more like a clown from Ringling Brothers!*

He barged into my office, leaned on the transom, and said, "Rick, I'm the new GM. My name is HB; ever heard of me?"

"No, can't say as I have," I responded.

This was the beginning of the end of my radio career. HB hired one of his DJ friends from upstate New York to be his informant on what employees were saying about him, and in this way, he created a reign of terror.

He owned a part-time business: he had an airplane and used it to tow banners for advertising. One of the first things he did when he arrived was pay a visit to our news director and ask her to do a story on his airborne-advertising business.

I find this totally outrageous. While working for my Fox television station in Phoenix, all employees were required to sign a statement that they were involved in no other businesses and would accept no money from anyone for any reason—that would be a conflict of interest and highly unethical. And *in no way* were we to use the station to broadcast anything for our own personal business or personal gain, which also would be highly unethical.

The Buffoon hated the brand-new love-songs format and wanted to change it to Top 40, not more than a couple of months after we'd changed to love songs. He wanted this not because the research showed it would be successful, but because, as he said over and over, "I like Top Forty. It's what I'm all about. I'm a Top Forty guy!" *I guess we're in the business to satisfy the whims of the boss*, I thought.

He also wanted to be back on the air, so he did an air shift on our AM, just to satisfy his ego. And what an ego he had. He was a megalomaniac, a self-absorbed narcissist. He also fired our consultant, John Lund, saying no one knew radio better than he.

The real problem was he thought he was God's gift to the world, to broadcasting, and especially to women, and he displayed it to all the girls on the staff. One day, in my presence, he cornered a female salesperson, and while speaking really softly to her, put his arm around her. With his other hand, he fondled her necklace.

Afterward, she came running into my office, crying. All the girls on the staff were scared to death of him. They complained to me and to the sales manager, George Faulk.

The sales manager and I complained to the human-resources director of the station's parent corporation, and guess what. The sales manager and I were fired!

Today, the Buffoon is no longer in any business related to radio, whereas I went on to a fifty-plus-year career in broadcasting, thanks to the ol' Buffoon. If he hadn't fired me, I never would have gone into TV.

Today when I speak to kids who want to get into broadcasting, they ask, "Why did you leave radio?"

And I respond, "I couldn't work there after what they said to me."

And they ask, "What was that?"

And I answer, "You're fired!"

And next, another miracle got me back into TV—this time for good.

21

GOD'S WILL, PLAN, AND PURPOSE FOR YOUR LIFE

It's when you discover what your God-given talents and abilities are that you discover why you are here and what your purpose is in life.

For some time, even before the Buffoon arrived, I had become increasingly disenchanted with radio. Can you imagine why? I was good on the creative side, but boy, putting up with all those characters was really against my grain. It just wasn't perfect for me!

I had been on television a number of times in the past, such as in my first job in Ashtabula and even anchoring in Battle Creek. I had appeared in a number of telethons and always got either offers or positive responses from television stations.

I was signed up with a talent agency, and they booked me a number of times for television commercials. On one occasion, I was in the studios of WILX-TV in Lansing doing a commercial, and I couldn't help but notice the news anchors getting ready for their evening newscast. The weatherman was a riot. He would run through the studios and offices making sounds like Curly from the Three Stooges. I thought, *He's having so much fun.* I said a prayer then and there: "God, please let me get into television."

(By the way, when I arrived at Channel 10 in Phoenix in the morning, some twenty-five years later, I would do the Curly thing when I walked in the door: whoop, whoop, whoop! It reminds me of that prayer.)

This story is also the subject of many speeches I've made in the past. It is a true story, but for some, it might be hard to believe. Here goes!

I was in a funk, and I didn't know what to do with my life. I was surfing the TV channels when I happened upon Pat Robertson, doing his annual *700 Club Telethon*, and he caught my attention.

Here's what Robertson said: "Most people want to know what their purpose is in life, and most people don't know. Everyone has been created by God with God-given talents and abilities, and each and every one is different. God gave some the ability and talent to be surgeons, others the ability to be lawyers or accountants, and others the ability to work with their hands or become artists—whatever. It's when you discover what your God-given talent and abilities are that you will discover why you are here and what your purpose is in life."

This was the answer I had sought. Over the years, I had been offered TV jobs, and many people had told me I should be in TV, but I'd always blown it off, thinking TV was not for me, but for actors or show-offs. Is this what the Lord was telling me to do? I wondered, *How do I know?*

I also, at the time, heard a presentation by Dr. Dennis Waitley, a renowned psychologist, who said most people don't know what their purpose is in life, and the only way to find out is to discover what their "natural" talents and abilities are. The only way to do this is to take an aptitude test to discover what you're good at. This was like a miracle happening in my life.

About this time, a friend of mine who was a psychologist called me out of the blue and asked how I was doing. God was working a miracle in my life again. I was ecstatic. I said, "Hey, are you familiar with those tests that tell you what your skills, talents, and abilities are?"

"Sure," he said. "Are you going through a midlife crisis?"

"No, no, not at all," I said. But I think it was my fourth!

We met in his office, he gave me the test, and I urged him to give me the results. "It's got to be mailed off and analyzed."

"When do I find out?"

"In a couple of weeks."

"Oh my God, I can't wait that long!"

A couple of weeks later, the time arrived. We met at a coffee shop. He looked across the table from me and said, "You won't believe the results!"

"What? Tell me!"

"Well, the number-one thing you should be doing in your life, according to the test is…" He began to laugh. He handed the paper to me across the table, pointing to the category. "Agriculture!"

"Agriculture! Is this a joke? Am I supposed to be a farmer?"

"No, it shows that you have an interest in the outdoors, the environment." And then he stopped laughing and got really excited. "But look at the second recommendation, vocal presentations; you have a talent in speaking to people. And there's more. When you combine the two, the job recommendation is…"—he sounded really excited then and turned the page—"TV weatherman!"

Can you believe this? Throughout my entire radio career—nineteen years and fifteen jobs—my very first job had come with TV. All those TV offers, and I'd ignored them. God had been telling me to be in TV, where I could possibly make a difference in people's lives, and I mostly ignored it, even quitting a TV job and turning down many others. Now I needed to get into TV, and I didn't quite know how to do it. So I prayed.

I prayed and prayed and prayed, and nothing happened.

One of my favorite TV preachers at that time was Fredrick Price, who wrote the book *Faith, Foolishness, or Presumption*. He said, "Faith is not enough; you have to act on what you believe." Problem was, I didn't know how to act; I just kept praying, and then the miracle happened.

I was getting fired. I knew it because the Buffoon took our morning DJ, Jack Robbins, out to lunch on a Friday. I called Jack that evening. "What did he say?" I asked.

"I hate this business," Jack replied.

What the heck kind of answer was that? "Did he say he was going to fire me?"

"I hate this business," Jack said over and over again. So much for my friend, whom I'd hired.

The following Monday came, and I was in my office. The door was closed. Someone knocked on the door. "Come in."

The Buffoon stuck his head in and asked, "Do you have this week's R&R?" (He meant the radio publication *Radio and Records*.)

"Nope," I answered. He closed the door. I had the *Lansing State Journal* newspaper spread out on my desk. A few minutes later, knock, knock on my door again. "Come in."

It's the Buffoon again. "Rick, can you come into my office?"

"Sure." I brought a yellow legal tablet to take notes, just to intimidate him.

He had his business manager sitting in the office with him; she was the HR person as well. I knew this was it. "Rick, we're going to let you go."

I started taking notes.

He said, "Well, if you want to take notes, we can too!" What an idiot.

I think he said the reason I was being fired was that I hadn't shown up at the station during a blizzard a few months earlier, even though the entire news department was there and was doing a good job, while I'd been stranded because my apartment was blocked by snowdrifts and I was waiting for the snowplows.

Anyway, that's the best he could do!

I walked back to my office, sat behind my desk, and rested my elbows on the newspaper spread out on my desk. Then I closed my eyes and prayed, "Lord, please help me." I opened my eyes and looked down at the paper. And there was an article staring me right in the face, written by the *Lansing State Journal*'s TV/radio reporter Mike Hughes. The headline read "WILX-TV loses two weathermen this week."

Two weather guys had left the station; the station had replaced one but needed to find another. This was a miracle. I picked up the phone without thinking. I called the station and asked for the news director, Ross Woodstock. I had met him in the past.

"Ross Woodstock speaking."

"Ross, this is Rick D'Amico calling. Are you looking for a weatherman?"

"Yeah!"

"How 'bout me?"

"When can you come down to the station?"

"How about right now?" I drove down to the station's studios, which were in Jackson, Michigan, about forty-five minutes south.

Ross knew me from my radio work and the telethons I had done on his station for Easter Seals. We talked, and he said, "You got the job."

I said, "Do I have to audition?"

"Nope, you got the job!"

I had prayed and prayed, but nothing had happened until I'd picked up the phone and acted on my faith. The Lord probably said, "Well, if you aren't going to do it, I'll push you along by getting you fired," which was a blessing—the best thing that ever happened in my career. It took a buffoon like the Huggy Bufoon to push me over the top and into a wonderful, lucrative career. He was an ass, but sometimes God will put these people in your life as a blessing, and it's difficult to recognize it unless you have faith. I remind myself of this every day.

So now I was a weatherman. But uh-oh, I knew nothing about doing the weather. Now what would I do?

22

MUNCHKINS GAWKING AT ME

There were little four-foot-tall munchkins all over the place gawking at me. Was it because I was the TV weatherman or just because I was a big-ass adult student in their little classroom?

I was driving home from WILX-TV, having just gotten the job as their weekend TV weatherman, and I was ecstatic. *Wait till I tell Ruth; she won't believe me*, I thought. I'd been fired from my radio job and hired by an NBC TV station on the same day!

Then, it was as if a black cloud came over me, a raging storm, distress, panic. *Oh my God!* I thought, *I don't know anything about weather.* Instead of driving home, I took an emergency detour, straight to the Lansing Public Library. A bespectacled librarian was sitting behind a desk.

"Hi!" I was excited and panicky at the same time. "I just got a job as a weatherman at Channel Ten!" I exclaimed. "Do you have any books on weather?"

She looked at me like I was crazy.

"I need the basic fundamentals, you know, like what it's all about."

I walked out of the library with *The Children's Golden Book of Weather*—a picture book.

Did the management of WILX-TV care or even ask if I knew anything about weather? No. It sounds just like getting that job in Ashtabula: in TV, it's not content that counts; it's talent. Performance is all that matters.

I loved my new job. I did the weather on weekends and filled in on weekdays; plus I did some fill-in news anchoring, and I had no idea what I was doing. I said stupid things like this: "This is a stationary front, which means it's not moving." And then, to cover up my ignorance, I would say, "Well, the only warm front I know is Shirley. I met her out in the parking lot!"

Because it was a part-time job, I also collected unemployment compensation from the state of Michigan. There were times when I would anchor the noon news and then run over to the unemployment office to get my weekly check. One day, as I stood in line, the unemployment lady at the counter said, "Didn't I just see you on the noon news?" People waiting in line for their unemployment checks asked me for my autograph.

WILX-TV was a strange station. It was actually intended to be a Jackson, Michigan, TV station; however, it wanted to be known as a Lansing television station. Its newsroom was in Lansing, while its studios were in Jackson, some forty miles south. All the news reporting and tape editing was done in Lansing, and in a frantic rush to get everything down to Jackson by deadline for the evening news, the team would throw the tapes into a big mailbag, and a different photographer each day drove them the forty-five minutes or more down to Jackson. Because of the harsh Michigan weather, both in summer and in the treacherous winters, the photographer many times would be late getting them to the studio in time for the newscasts.

It would be ten minutes until the start of the six o'clock news. "News studio to shuttle, over," the news anchor would frantically call for the tapes for his newscast.

"This is shuttle; go ahead."

"Tell me you're almost here."

"OK, I'm almost there!"

"Seriously, where the hell are you?"

"I'm twenty minutes out, and I can't go any faster; the roads are all ice."

"Oh my God."

Then the anchor would begin the newscast. "Good evening. In the news tonight, a daring midday bank robbery in downtown Lansing. Brad Goode has the story." Long pause. Nothing would happen. "We'll try and have that story in a minute." This would go on for about ten minutes—reporters' stories had not arrived yet. Finally, the photographer would rush into the control room and dump the mailbag upside down. All the reporters' tapes would crash to the floor, and a big rush was on to find the next one to go on the air.

The Channel 10 job was part-time. I was making about fifty bucks a show, so with my unemployment money, I was pulling down only about $400 a week. I needed to work full-time. So after a few months, a full-time, prime-time weather job opened up at Channel 6, the CBS station across town. I had no contract, so I applied for the job with news director Jim Bliecher, who hired me right away.

During my two-week notice, I would sit in the Channel 10 newsroom and see promos on Channel 6 about me going there to do the weather. Unbelievable!

The Channel 10 news director was livid when I quit. Throwing an ashtray at me, he screamed, "I had big plans for you!" And the general manager, Ron Kwasnick, was incensed that I would go to work for the competition.

Now I was doing the weather on WLNS, Channel 6 CBS, the big gun in town. I had been on the air doing the weather for about six months, and I was so worried about not knowing anything about weather that I decided to enroll in a meteorology class. Michigan State University had none, so I found one at Lansing Community College. I called the professor. "Hi, this is Rick D'Amico calling."

"Hey, Rick, I watch you all the time!"

"Oh, thanks," I said. "I'd like to take your class, Meteorology 101."

A long pause followed. "You're kidding?"

"Nope!"

Another long pause. "Well, we'd love to have you."

"Do you need any math to take this course?" I asked.

"Well, yes, you need at least basic algebra."

"No problem," I said. I was lying. I'd never had algebra, never had anything but stupid-math class in high school. (Math for dumb kids!) Panic again struck my brain. *How do I learn algebra really fast?* I saw an ad in the paper for Sylvan Learning Center, a school that tutors children who are weak in education fundamentals. So I took a deep breath and gave them a call. "Hi, this is Rick D'Amico calling."

"Hi, Rick, I watch you all the time!" Here we go again.

I was sitting in a classroom with coat hooks that were three feet high on the wall, in a tiny chair, with my knees up to my chin, and a nice lady was teaching me algebra. There were little four-foot-tall munchkins all over the place gawking at me. Was it because I was the TV weatherman or just because I was a big-ass adult student in their little classroom? But hey, I learned algebra and was ready to go to college.

On my first day in Meteorology 101 at Lansing Community College, the students saw me and said, "Hey, it's Rick D'Amico, our TV weatherman! Are you teaching this class?"

"No, I'm here to learn."

We went on a field trip to the National Weather Service one day. The meteorologist in charge was standing at the door and asked, "Hey, Rick D'Amico, are you the professor?"

"No, I'm a student!"

Channel 6 WLNS was the CBS station, formerly WJIM-TV in Lansing. Here's what I remember about Channel 6: The building was shaped like a Holiday Inn. It had a courtyard with a swimming pool. The story goes that the former owner, Hal Gross, had named the station after his son, Jim, and he didn't know for sure if the TV business would work out. If it didn't, he could always convert it into a motel.

Everyone loved the swimming pool. In between the six and the eleven o'clock news, employees would have their families come over for barbecue and swimming. It was really wonderful, but not for long.

A few months after I arrived, the station was sold to Young Broadcasting. A sophomoric kid in a three-piece suit held a meeting. His name was Vincent Young, and he was the new boss, another guy who made it big by working for his father. He talked to the employees about how great their company was. Weeks later, they drained the pool. We all hated the company and him after that.

The new owner of Channel 6 hired a new general manager—Ron Kwasnick. Yep, the general manager of Channel 10 who was incensed that I would leave his precious station to go work for Channel 6!

Ruth and I bought a beautiful house in the Groesbeck area of Lansing. It was a lovely two-story colonial with a big backyard with apple trees and was very close to Channel 6.

My weather career was thriving. I was putting to good use the knowledge I was gaining from my college class; the station was number one, and everything was just fine. All this time, Ruth had held on to her job in Battle Creek at the Battle Creek Equipment Company. Her bosses loved her and kept giving her raises every time they thought she might leave. But commuting ninety miles one way from Battle Creek to Lansing was getting to be a real chore.

And then it happened. One day I came home after the six o'clock news to find her making a wonderful dinner of shrimp and lobster. We sat down at the dinner table, and she had tears in her eyes.

"I'm pregnant," she said. This was our third pregnancy. We already had two girls, and I was hoping for a boy, so this was good news for both of us.

We were very happy, but I knew I had to find another job so Ruth could stay home with the children.

23

A MULTIPLE BIRTH

During the delivery, the medical staff in the delivery room kept asking me about the TV business. Ruth was in pain, and I was bragging about my job.

Ruth had to pee really badly, but she couldn't, because she was flat on her back in a hospital examination room about to get an amniocentesis. She was thirty-five years old, and her doctor had suggested the test to make sure there were no abnormalities.

The ultrasound technician put gel on Ruth's stomach and moved the wand around. "Uh-oh!" the technician exclaimed.

"What's wrong?" I asked, getting scared.

"Oh my!" she said. "Did anyone mention anything to you about a multiple birth?"

"Multiple birth? How many are in there?" I was gasping for air.

Ruth was pregnant with twins! The ultrasound technician blurted, "Oh, I just noticed something—they're boys!" Words cannot explain how happy, excited, and in awe we were of how God works in our lives. It was a wonderful, miraculous blessing.

Sal and Mario were born one hour apart. During the delivery, the medical staff in the delivery room kept asking me about the TV business. Ruth was in pain, and I was bragging about my job. I was having a hard time concentrating because they had me holding an oxygen mask in case Ruth needed it. I thought I might need to save her life at any moment. It turns out it was not connected to anything; they were just trying to keep me from passing out.

After the boys were born, life became a real hassle. Ruth went back to work, a babysitter took care of Sal and Mario for part of the day, my two daughters were in school, and I was working 3:00 p.m. to about midnight in order to do the six and eleven o'clock news. I was making about $30,000 a year. Ruth was making about the same, and I thought, *I have to find a real job that pays me at least that much so Ruth can be a full-time mom.*

Enter the agent who went to prison!

24

ANYWHERE IT DOESN'T SNOW

"Where do you want to live?" he asked.
"Anywhere it doesn't snow," I replied. "I hate
snow, and I hate cold!"

By this time, I was established pretty well as a popular TV weatherman in Lansing, Michigan. The number-one radio station in town, WFMK-FM, had also hired me to do the weather on their number-one morning show, which I did out of a studio they built in my basement. This was not as cool or convenient as it sounds.

It was a challenge because my dog at the time, Smokey, who was part collie and part German shepherd, would bark every time he heard me on the air.

David J. Bennett, the morning DJ, would interrupt and ask, "What's that barking all about?"

"That's Smokey the weather dog; he's calling for rain!"

Then the twins would start crying, and it was just chaotic. Ruth would yell downstairs, "What do you want for breakfast?"

"Ruth, I'm on the air, for heaven's sake!" Tons of laughter would ensue—on the air.

Bennett was always getting offers from big-time radio stations from around the country. "How's that happening for you?" I asked.

"I have an agent; he's fantastic!"

I signed up with the agent, Saul. He was very aggressive and outspoken. I never met the man; all our conversations were on the phone.

"Where do you want to live?" he asked.

"Anywhere it doesn't snow," I replied. "I hate snow, and I hate cold!"

The winter was especially rough that year. One of our reporters, Don West, would come in from an assignment, all bundled up, with hat, scarf, and moon boots, icicles hanging from his nose, just frozen to death. I spent a lot of time kidding him about how he couldn't take the snow and the cold. "Hey, I'm from Arizona," he would cry.

"Oh yeah? Where in Arizona?"

"A little town outside Phoenix called Tempe."

"What's it like living there?"

"Just amazing—warm year-round, and they have a couple of great TV stations."

He talked about NewsCenter 10 in Phoenix, a big station with a helicopter, satellite truck, live trucks, and great talent on the air. I thought, *Sounds good*, but I never gave a thought to Arizona as a place to live.

You should have seen the look on Don's face when he struggled in from the cold one day and there was a NewsCenter 10 coffee mug on his desk. Hint—I put it there.

25

CAN YOU ADJUST TO LIVING IN THE DESERT?

...manicured green grass, palm trees, sprinklers watering the flowers, and orange trees with real oranges hanging from them—the temperature was in the eighties. "This is paradise!"

Lansing, Michigan, has about seventy sunny days a year. This does not take into account partly cloudy days; add those to the cloudy, and you get about *twenty* sunny days. The city is on the lee side of Lake Michigan, meaning the prevailing winds and weather systems usually roar in from the west and south; the lake's moisture creates a lot of clouds and bad weather. Plus, this area of the country is known by climatologists as the crossroads of storms in the United States. You know the old saying, "If you don't like the weather, just wait a few minutes"? I think it originated in Lansing.

On this day, it was particularly nasty. An ice storm was devastating the city. I drove up to the parking lot of Channel 6, turned off the ignition, and huddled in my car. *I can't get out of the car!* I thought. *It's too cold.* But I took a deep breath and ran across the parking lot; the ice was hitting my face like buckshot, and by the time I got into the station, icicles were forming on my nose.

I made it to the weather office. A note on my phone said, "Call your agent."

Saul was in a good mood. "A news director is going to call you tonight when you get home from the six o'clock news. His name is Dave Howell. He's the news boss at KTSP-TV in Phoenix, Arizona," he said.

"Where the heck is Phoenix?" I asked.

"It's where it doesn't snow, remember? Now, be polite and positive. Answer his questions, and don't talk about money; that's my job. If he likes what he hears, he'll invite you to fly in for an interview."

Once the six o'clock news was over, I ran out of the studio, grabbed my overcoat, and rushed out to the parking lot…where my car was covered with about two inches of ice. Quickly, I grabbed the windshield scraper and frantically started banging the ice off my car. I couldn't care less if the paint came off; I had to get home for that phone call!

I couldn't eat. I was pacing by the phone, wondering, *Will it really ring?*

It did. It was him. Howell was a very nice, articulate-sounding guy. He asked me a few questions, told me he liked my tape, and wanted to know if I could fly down for an interview. Then he asked, "Do you think you'll have any problems adjusting to living in the desert southwest?"

I took a deep breath and said, "I just scraped two inches of ice off my car; are you kidding?"

It was December, and I was in the middle of a whiteout; the snow was coming down so hard, I couldn't see two feet in front of me, and to make matters worse, the wind was blowing about thirty miles an hour. So add a blizzard to the whiteout, and it means I was standing outside my car at a gas station trying to fill up the tank, but the wind and snow were blowing so hard in my face that I had to turn the other way. I couldn't figure out why it was taking so long. The temperature was about twenty degrees, but the wind chill was well below zero. Finally, I looked over and realized I was pumping gas on the ground because I couldn't see. For those of you who have never lived in the Midwest, let me tell you a whiteout is God punishing humans for their sins.

This happened when I was trying to drive to the airport to fly to Phoenix for my job interview. I remember when the plane finally got over Arizona. Flights to Phoenix from the east usually fly over the northern part of Arizona and head south into Phoenix. Looking out the window, all I could see was what appeared to be the surface of the moon. Desolate brown dirt everywhere, rocks and mountains, and I couldn't find a sign that humans inhabited the land down there.

Then houses came into view. Their roofs were all covered with orange tile, and when the plane landed at Sky Harbor International Airport, the sun was so bright, the mountains so magnificent, and the buildings so clean. And the palm trees—oh my God, this was what I'd always dreamed of.

Doug Drew met me at the gate. Drew was the assistant news director of KTSP, Channel 10, and one of the nicest guys I've ever met in the business. Drew would go on in later years to distinguish himself as being one of the brightest minds in TV-morning-show programming. As a consultant today, he has clients all around the world.

Drew drove me to the station, and as we left the airport, the first thing I noticed was manicured green grass, palm trees, sprinklers watering the flowers, and orange trees with real oranges hanging from them; the temperature was in the eighties. "This is paradise!" I said to Drew, and he laughed.

A billboard at the entrance to the highway leading to the station was for a TV station's news department. And the big anchor on the billboard was Dave Patterson. Patterson was one of my idols from Cleveland television. "Dave Patterson works here in Phoenix?" I asked.

"Yeah, at our station!" Drew replied.

"Wow, I'm going to work with Dave Patterson? Wait until my mom hears about this!" I said. To me, this was the big time.

And what do you suppose was the first question the general manager asked in my job interview?

26

YOU GOT A POOL?

His face was red, icicles hung from his earmuffs, and snow hugged his moon boots. He looked at his desk, saw the coffee mug, and was shocked.

The job interview consisted of breakfast at a downtown Phoenix hotel; Dave Howell, the news director, and Bill Stough, the general manager, of KTSP-TV sat across from me.

The GM opened the conversation. "So I understand you guys got a pool there at your station in Lansing?"

Can you imagine my shock when he asked this? "Yes! How'd you know that?" I asked.

"Your old GM, who left when the station was sold, is my best friend. He said he wanted to adopt you." I guess I didn't have to worry much about getting the job after that.

So here we go again, with someone who knew me and vouched for me to a prospective boss. The people you meet along the way and how you treat them will affect your success in life.

I flew back to Lansing the following morning. I'd had a fun dinner the night before with Howell; the number-one weather guy at the station, Dave Munsey; and the weekend meteorologist, Jim Schnebelt. Dave

Munsey, by the way, is right up there in the top of the funniest guys I've ever met in my life. He had a joke just about every three minutes, and we laughed and ate and had a really wonderful time.

The station's promotion department made sure I had plenty of Newscenter 10 T-shirts and coffee mugs to take home.

The following afternoon, when I arrived at work at WLNS in Lansing, I placed a KTSP Newscenter 10 mug on Don West's desk. (He was the reporter from Tempe, Arizona, who couldn't stand the Michigan winters.)

West came walking into the newsroom after being out in the harsh winter weather; his face was red, icicles hung from his earmuffs, and snow hugged his moon boots. He looked at his desk, saw the coffee mug, and was shocked. "Where did you get this?" he asked.

"I was there this weekend for a job interview."

"How'd that happen?"

"I don't know. My agent sent out one tape, just one, to them, and they invited me in for an interview."

"Did you get the job?"

"I don't know; I think so. They're going to call me after the holidays."

"I hope to go back someday," he said sadly.

Don West, by the way, did go back to Phoenix, and he went on to be the executive director of the Arizona State Fair. It was a huge job, and he was very good at it. He is now retired and living in San Diego—no icicles hanging from his nose there.

And thanks to a future prisoner, I got the job!

27

YEAH, BUT HE'S IN PRISON!

"I hate that SOB. I sued him, and I won;
he's an ass!"
I was stunned.

"Do you have an agent?" New reporters and interns asked me that question all the time.

"Yeah, but he's in prison." It always got a laugh, as though I had made it up.

Saul Foos, in my opinion, was an amazing agent. He was firm and a good negotiator, and he really stood up for his clients—perhaps he was just *too* good.

When Dave Howell, the KTSP news director, put me on the plane to fly back to Lansing, he told me he would call after the holidays with his decision. So I had the month of December to sweat it out.

The week after the holidays, on Monday morning, Saul called. "Have you heard anything yet?"

"Nope."

"I talked with Howell, and they're going to call you today or tomorrow. Now, listen. When he talks about money, tell him you can't talk about that. Just tell him that's my job. OK?"

"Got it. Don't worry."

Dave Howell called the following day. "Rick, I'd like to offer you a job!"

"Great," I said.

"We would like you to come on board with us doing the noon and 6:00 p.m. weather. We'll pay for you and your wife to fly down here on a house-hunting trip, we'll pay all your relocation expenses, and we'll give you a five-year deal starting at fifty thousand dollars a year!"

"Oh, well, I can't talk money; that's for my agent, Saul," I gingerly suggested.

"Well, that's going to be a problem," Howell said. "You see, our general manager hates him—can't stand him—and won't have anything to do with him at all."

I was in shock. I thanked Howell and told him I'd get back to him right away, and then I got on the phone and frantically called Saul.

He was incensed. "Who's the general manager?"

"Bill Stough," I answered.

Saul started screaming in the phone. "I hate that SOB. I sued him, and I won; he's an ass."

I was stunned. I was thinking, of all the general managers and all the agents in the United States of America, why do I have to be between these two guys who hate each other at the time of my big break?

I negotiated the deal myself, with Saul's advice. After I signed the deal, Ruth and I flew down to Phoenix and found a home to rent in Glendale. Ruth fell in love with Arizona immediately.

During the first few months I was working in Phoenix, Saul would call and ask how Ruth was and how the family was doing, and then he would suggest we get his fee in right away. I paid him monthly—7 percent of my first year's income, and 5 percent of every year for the rest of the contract.

Why was Saul calling every month to urge me to send him his fee? Well, as many newspapers reported afterward, he had set up an investment program for his rich clients (I wasn't included), and instead of investing the money, he spent it on himself. It was a classic Ponzi scheme, in which he bilked his clients out of $7.2 million. He went to prison. Saul Foos died in 2012, broke and a broken man, according to Chicago news stories.

"Hey, Rick, do you have an agent?"

"Yeah, but he's in prison!"

"Oh, Rick, you're so funny!"

28

WHATEVER HAPPENED TO TWO WEEKS' NOTICE?

He opened his bottom left-hand desk drawer,
and there was a bottle of whisky and a couple
of cups. He said, "Do you want a drink?"
I was shocked. "Ah, no, I don't think so; I have
to go on the air in a few minutes."

My contract at Channel 6 in Lansing called for me to give three months' notice. I knew that once I gave my notice, they would either try to talk me out of leaving or fire me. They did both.

Ron Kawsnick, the general manager, invited me into his office. "Let's sit on the couch, Rick," he said as he offered me a cup of coffee from a coffee bar near his desk.

I declined but sat on one end of the couch; he sat on the other. "I want you to think about this," he began. "You have a beautiful house here in Lansing. You have four children, you just had twins, and you have to think about the security of your family." He was talking but not looking at me. "Think how risky it is to take a job all the way across the country, with an unknown company. Now, I want you to stay, and I'm willing to give you a big pay increase if you do. How much money do you want to stay here?"

He was paying me $30,000 a year. The new job in Phoenix was paying me $50,000 a year, with good increases over five years. This, by the way, was not bad in 1987. Plus, KTSP in Phoenix was one of the top television-news operations in the country, number one in the Southwest; it was more than money—it was a wonderful opportunity in the big time.

I looked him square in the eyes and said, "Eighty thousand dollars a year."

"Oh my God." Honestly, I thought he was going to have a heart attack. "Oh my God, we can never pay you that! Eighty thousand dollars a year? Oh my God, no, no." His pudgy face was beet-red, and he was hyperventilating.

I didn't say a word; the ball was in his court. He regained his composure and said, "Listen, this is what I'm going to do for you. You go home, talk to your wife and kids, and think it over. Call me at nine o'clock tomorrow morning and tell me you're going to stay, and I'll make it right for you."

What did that mean: "Make it right for you?" I didn't know, but I left his office. Do you suppose he thought $80,000 a year was asking for too much? I don't know, but I do know this: when he left Young Broadcasting, he got a bonus of $2 million.

I didn't call him the next morning. I didn't call him at all. That evening, around eight o'clock, the phone rang. I answered. "Rick, this is Ron; have you made a decision?"

"I'm going to Phoenix," I said.

"Going for the money, huh?" he asked.

"Yep, you got that right," I answered.

I didn't particularly like this man for two reasons. One, he had drained the pool. Two, when he took over as GM, he had asked all employees to fill out an application form and reapply to the company for employment. I scribbled in big letters across the form: "READ MY CONTRACT!" He called me into his office when he received it and said, "We'll honor your contract," like he was doing me a favor.

When my agent gave them my three months' notice, he told them that if they let me go before the three months were over, they'd have to pay me for the entire three months. That sounds fair, seeing as they put it in their contract to hold me for three months, which would make it hard to find a job requiring the new employer to wait three months.

They called me in the office and told me I could work out two weeks' notice and leave. I agreed. In the meantime, Saul fixed it up for me to have KTSP in Phoenix put me on their payroll immediately.

A week into my two weeks' notice, during the 11:00 p.m. news, I noticed the Channel 6 news director, Bruce Cornelius, sitting in his office. That never happened, especially not during the eleven o'clock news. After the newscast, he called me into his office and fired me. What a classy operation that was.

Cornelius was a crusty, old-school journalist, who had cut his eyeteeth as a photographer for the *Lansing State Journal*. He used to call me in the office, and the first thing he would say to me was, "You asshole!" I think he meant this affectionately. One day, he called and said, "Get in my office."

I walked in, and after the usual greeting, he said to sit down. I did. He opened his bottom left-hand desk drawer, and there was a bottle of whisky and a couple of cups. He said, "Do you want a drink?"

I was shocked. "Ah, no, I don't think so; I have to go on the air in a few minutes."

"I don't like the color of your weather maps," he said.

"OK, I'll change them."

"OK, get the hell out of here!"

I left.

About three years later, I was sitting in the weather office at Channel 10 in Phoenix when the phone rang. I answered, "Rick D'Amico speaking."

On the other end, I heard a familiar voice: "You asshole."

"Hi, Bruce!" I was happy to hear his voice. He just wanted to talk. He was a good guy.

I had some fun memories of Channel 6 in Lansing. One afternoon before going on the air, we were horsing around in the office, and we were late getting to the anchor desk for the 6:00 p.m. news opening. The news intro started, and we were running to the set. I was wearing a blue blazer with gold buttons, and so was the male anchor, Mike Redford. We always hung our jackets on coat hooks just outside the news set. Mike was about six feet tall, while I was five foot five. We grabbed each other's jackets, and when the 6:00 p.m. news started, I was sitting there with a jacket about five sizes too big, and Mike was sitting there saying, "Good evening, ladies and gentlemen," with my jacket on, and about three feet of his naked arms were protruding out from his sleeves. It was a riot; we laughed through the whole show.

I also remember Jane Aldrich, who was an amazing news anchor and a beautiful, intelligent, and most gracious person. She stayed at Channel 6 for a long time and became a legend in Lansing. As I write this, she is still anchoring the news on Channel 6, although she has announced she will retire in a few months.

And I do remember something really odd about working there. As I mentioned earlier, WLNS was previously WJIM-TV. During its heyday, it called itself Newscenter 6, and it ran a station break that said, "Blessed is the nation whose god is the Lord." At the same time, KTSP in Phoenix, the station I was going to, was owned by Phoenix businessman Tom Chauncey, and he ran the same IDs. At the time, Hal Gross, a part-time resident of a wealthy suburb of Phoenix, owned WJIM in Lansing.

The older employees of the station, when they found out I was going to KTSP in Phoenix, were excited to tell me Channel 6 was patterned after Channel 10. So the fact that I was going from Newscenter 6 in Lansing, Michigan, to Newscenter 10 in Phoenix, Arizona, was special to them and to me. It was strange, almost like divine intervention—another miracle?

So I was on my way to Phoenix to be a weatherman, but never in a million years did I think I would be doing the weather coast to coast on national television.

29

PHOENIX, ARIZONA

A doctor wearing cowboy boots! We had never seen anything like that before.

Ruth and I packed our entire family into our Ford minivan and drove across the country. We had six-month-old twins, a four-year-old daughter, a sixteen-year-old daughter, and our sedated dog.

Our first night was in Terre Haute, Indiana. A basketball team was also staying at our hotel; go figure.

The second night was in Springfield, Missouri. Ruth came running out of a gas station all excited. "I just saw two guys in there wearing cowboy hats!"

The third night was in Amarillo, Texas. My two sons, Sal and Mario, had developed ear infections, and they cried most of the time—a relaxing drive, that was. We checked into a Holiday Inn and hid the fact that we had a dog with us. There was some kind of power failure, so there were no lights. Smokey barked like crazy, and the boys were crying. I thought we were going to get kicked out of the hotel.

We went to a doctor the next day to have the boys checked out. I was wearing an Everlast sweatshirt. While the doctor was examining the boys, Ruth nudged me and looked down at his feet. He was wearing cowboy boots. A doctor wearing cowboy boots! We had never seen anything like that before. When we were leaving, the doctor asked me, "Are you a prize fighter?"

"Me? No, I'm a TV weatherman!" I guess Everlast sportswear hadn't made it that far west yet. (Everlast originally was a company that began by developing equipment for boxing.)

The fourth night was in Gallup, New Mexico. All I remember from this stop is a lot of mud and a bunch of people walking around with nothing to do.

On the fifth day, we arrived in Phoenix. It was in January and the most beautiful day—sunny, not a cloud in the sky; the temperature was in the eighties.

When the movers finished unloading all our belongings in our new home in Glendale, I couldn't help but notice a couple of items that sat tall in the garage: two ice scrapers and a snow shovel.

And now I was working for a former president's family!

30

CHANNEL 10

One morning, at around 10:00 a.m., there was a breaking news story, and there were no anchors in the building.

Channel 10 at the time was KTSP-TV, and it belonged to Taft Television and Radio, a company owned by the Taft family of Ohio—you know, the one that produced the president and governor and other politicians? It was a good company with a good reputation.

The station had more viewers than all the other stations in town, and it had a rich history. One day, after parking my car and walking up to the entrance of the station, I noticed two huge gates at the opening of the alley that separated the two buildings it occupied. On the gates was a huge letter *A* with wings on each side of the letter. This stood for the Flying A Ranch, owned by Gene Autry, the legendary singing cowboy of movies and TV, and one of my boyhood heroes. He was a previous owner, along with local businessman Tom Chauncy.

The station also had the most talented news anchors in Phoenix. Dave Patterson, Debra Pyburn, and weatherman Dave Munsey did the 5:00 and 10:00 p.m. news. Bill Close and Claren Scott anchored the noon and 6:00 p.m. newscasts, on which I was the weatherman.

Dave Patterson was an extremely articulate, intelligent, and knowledgeable news anchor, whose talent and intelligence far exceeded the needs of television news. He was one of my idols in Cleveland, Ohio, when I was starting my career, and I always thought it was an honor to work with him. I coanchored election-night coverage with him one year, and it was a highlight.

Bill Close was a legend in Phoenix television news. By the time I arrived at Channel 10, he'd been demoted from news director to main anchor and then anchor of the noon and 6:00 p.m. news. During Bill's management days, he was an extremely hard-driving, no-nonsense boss. My days with him were just wonderful. He was a grammarian; he insisted you speak in perfect English. And you had to show him you weren't intimidated by him.

One day during a break in the 6:00 p.m. news, he told me about the grapefruit trees in the yard around his house. I asked him, "Where are you at?"

He replied, "You just ended a sentence with a preposition." He had that gruff look on his face.

I said, "I'm sorry. Where are you at—asshole?"

He looked at me with a horrible, mean look on his face, then burst out laughing. He liked me; I liked him.

Bill passed away on January 27, 2013. Months before he died, he visited the station, I don't think he recognized me.

Dave Munsey is one of the funniest people I've had the pleasure to work with. In my time in the weather office working with him, we would sit there, he would tell jokes and we would and laugh and laugh and laugh.

I got in every morning at 9:00 a.m.; put my weather together, with my forecasting and maps; did my three minutes on the noon news; and went home for a couple of hours. I came back at three thirty in the afternoon, put maps together for the 6:00 p.m., and then went home for the day.

Channel 10 agreed to pay for my further meteorology education, and I enrolled in the Mississippi State Broadcast Meteorology Program, where I was in the school's first graduating class.

I've always had the mind-set that anything management asks me to do, I'll do. Being in broadcast management in the past, I know how difficult it is to deal with temperamental talent, and I always wanted to be the go-to guy.

I remember the day Pope John Paul II was visiting Phoenix in 1987, my first year at Channel 10. We covered just about every second of it. The entire news staff was on duty. My job: do the weather. The producer cued me from the booth. "You're next. Do about three minutes."

I was in place, and just seconds before the weather intro rolled, the producer said the pope was about to speak. Dave Patterson and Debra Pyburn announced, "Let's go live now to Pope John Paul the Second."

They killed my weather, so I turned off my mike and walked into the lunchroom. Rolland Smith, CBS news anchor, who was there covering the event for CBS, looked at me with a big smile. "It's a historical event in your career, Rick."

"What's that?" I asked.

"You've just been preempted by the pope!" Rolland Smith brought home the point that what we do is insignificant compared to people in our world who are truly making a difference. I liked him.

One morning, at around 10:00 a.m., there was a breaking news story, and there were no anchors in the building. Assistant news director Doug Drew came to me and asked, "Can you anchor?"

"Of course," I replied.

"Get on the anchor desk," he said.

I guess I was good, because they asked me to continue to anchor when they needed me. I began filling in anchoring the noon news at times and doing headline newsbreaks while still keeping my weather duties.

One of the highlights of my entire career came in what I thought was a prank phone call.

31

THE SHOW

"I watched you every morning. You'd be great filling in for our CBS weatherman, Mark McEwen, when he goes on vacation."

In the eighties, the broadcast networks ruled the roost. NBC, ABC, and CBS were the big time—"the Show," as they say in Major League Baseball. If you worked at a local station, your goal was always to go to the network. It was where all the money and prestige were. To be seen and heard from coast to coast was dying and going to heaven.

Channel 10, at the time, and for the longest part of its history, was a CBS affiliate, and an important one. It led the nation in delivering one of the largest audience shares to the *CBS Evening News* with Walter Cronkite and later Dan Rather.

I had been reassigned to cohosting and doing the weather on a new Channel 10 morning show, called *Daybreak*. My coanchor was Linda Williams, one of the nicest, warmest friends I've had in broadcasting, and to this day I cherish our conversations together. We were just yukking it up, doing the news and the weather for a half hour before the *CBS Morning News* and *CBS This Morning* began. We were number-one rated and having a ball.

Before voice mail and cell phones, there were those little "You Were Called By" pink slips that someone would place on your phone if you got a phone call.

One day, there was one sitting on my phone. "You were called by CBS!" it said. "Please return the call." I did, thinking it was a prank, probably by Dave Munsey or some jokester in the newsroom.

It was John Goodman, a senior producer of *CBS This Morning*, and he wanted to know if I'd be interested in coming to New York City to fill in doing the weather on the *CBS Morning News* and *CBS This Morning*.

"Is this a joke?" I asked.

He laughed. "No, I was on vacation at the Boulders in Carefree, and I watched you every morning. You'd be great filling in for our CBS weatherman, Mark McEwen, when he goes on vacation."

I was ecstatic and overwhelmed. Everyone at the station was congratulating me, and my relatives in Cleveland, Ohio, were all excited; they were going to see their Richey on national TV.

General Manager Ron Bergamo called me in his office and said, "We don't want to make this too big of a deal, because Dave Munsey will get embarrassed."

I said, "No way—Dave and I are friends; he doesn't see it that way. I do the morning show; it's a morning-show thing."

Bergamo was always seen as something like a used-car salesman; he was always trying to manipulate rather than motivate. He used to leave what seemed like hour-long voice messages to tell us what was going on in the station.

Anyway, back to CBS. I got the call, and it was legit. I was on my way to "*the* Show."

32

NEW YORK, NEW YORK

Harry Smith was ad-libbing into the camera,
"And I'm here with Paula Zahn; Connie Chung;
Chris Matthews; the Reverend Jesse Jackson;
and from our CBS affiliate in Phoenix, Arizona,
weatherman Rick D'Amico."

Ruth and I arrived at John F. Kennedy International Airport in New York City on a Sunday afternoon. While hopping in a cab, we immediately noticed a New York police officer yelling at a cabbie to move his car. "Now!" he screamed.

The drive across Queens and into Manhattan was exhilarating. It was a beautiful summer day. We checked into the Essex House on Central Park and took a walk around the city. *Just like in the movies!* I thought.

We were hungry and found a Houlihan's Irish bar and restaurant in the Chrysler Building. We had dinner and went back to the hotel room. I had to go to bed early, because I was waking up at 3:30 a.m. (12:30 a.m. Arizona time)!

The phone in our hotel room rang at 4:30 a.m. It was the front desk. "Mr. D'Amico, your car is here."

As I stepped off the elevator, I saw a man in a black hat and black suit. "Mr. D'Amico?"

I nodded.

"Right this way." He led me to the front of the hotel and opened the back door to a black Lincoln Town Car. I climbed in, and we were off to the CBS Broadcast Center on West Fifty-Seventh Street. CBS sent a car for me every morning. There never was a car for me after the show; I walked back to our hotel room. I guess CBS just wanted to make sure I got to work on time.

When I was growing up in the fifties and sixties, most television came out of New York City. I watched the news with Douglas Edwards, Charles Collingwood, Harry Reasoner, and Walter Cronkite, and never in a million years did I ever think I would be, someday, in the same studio in New York, broadcasting. And here I was!

I stepped out of the car in front of the CBS Broadcast Center, and I thought this was a crappy part of town; I later learned it was a *good* part of town, because most of Manhattan is kind of crappy by clean Phoenix, Arizona, standards.

Walking through the front door, I immediately noticed a large plaque with the image of Edward R. Murrow and an inscription about journalism ethics and how the building and news operation were dedicated to him and his values. I was beginning to hyperventilate.

The chief meteorologist, George Cullen, welcomed me. He was the nicest guy. His role was that of behind-the-scenes producer. He took me up to the weather office, which was next door to Andy Rooney's office.

He gave me a weather briefing, and he was hilarious. We grabbed a bagel and coffee in the CBS commissary, and he hustled me into the elevator and upstairs to makeup. Afterward, he escorted me into the big CBS news studio. (On one of these later trips on the CBS elevator with George Cullen, the elevator door opened, and in walked the legendary Mike Wallace—trench coat and all, sipping a coffee in a to-go cup. He nodded good morning, and I was speechless.)

OK, so now I was in the studio, ready to go on the air for the first time on the CBS television network. *Oh my God!* I was thinking, *This is the studio of Murrow, Edwards, Reasoner, Cronkite, and Rather; what am I doing here?*

A man with a bow tie was sitting at the anchor desk. "Hi, Rick, I'm Charles Osgood. It's wonderful to meet you."

I was about to throw up; I was so nervous. I was anchoring with Charles Osgood, and I was about to do the weather on CBS, coast to coast, to the entire United States of America.

Something strange happened when I went on the air. I can be, at times, nervous beforehand, but when the camera is on, a calm comes over me and I just become me.

So I did the weather, without incident—which means I didn't pass out—on the *CBS Morning News* and was hustled into the *CBS This Morning* studio. Now I was really dealing with nerves. Harry Smith introduced himself, along with Connie Chung, Paula Zahn, Chris Matthews, and the Reverend Jesse Jackson.

CBS This Morning was called "the big show." It was on the air from 7:00 to 9:00 a.m. with news, weather, and guests and topics ranging from serious issues of the day to the best toothpaste.

I did the weather on the hour and half hour immediately after the newscasts. Cullen stood next to me, off camera, to brief me and probably to ensure I didn't collapse.

I did a good job—so good, in fact, that one of the producers asked if I would like to sit in on the "Co-Op."

"Sure, I'd love to; what's the Co-Op?" I asked.

"It's a five-minute segment at twenty-five past the hour, where you just sit around on the kitchen set and talk about anything that comes to mind," he responded.

"OK," I meekly replied. I was thinking, *Now I'm really going to make an ass out of myself!*

"It's twenty-five past the hour." We were coming out of a commercial break, we were on the air, and Harry Smith was ad-libbing into the camera, "And I'm here with Paula Zahn; Connie Chung; Chris Matthews; the

Reverend Jesse Jackson; and from our CBS affiliate in Phoenix, Arizona, weatherman Rick D'Amico."

He looked over to Matthews and said, "Chris, you just got back from Northern Ireland; what's happening there?"

Beep, beep, beep—an alarm was going off in the back of my mind. *They're talking about Northern Ireland,* I was thinking. *What the heck am I going to talk about if the conversation comes my way?* Matthews talked about the unrest in Northern Island and the politics, and then he stopped. Oh no—a lull in the conversation. Harry Smith looked over to me. He smiled and asked, "Rick, have you ever been to Ireland?"

There was a pause, and then I responded, "No, but last night I ate at Houlihan's"

Then a longer pause. Smith looked into the camera and said, "We'll be back in just a moment."

Later that day, as Ruth and I walked down Madison Avenue, we noticed a tall woman with dark hair, crossing the street with a small entourage of about four people. The lady looked at me; it was Jacqueline Kennedy Onassis! She looked away, then looked back at me and nodded, as if to say hello.

"Oh my God—that's Jackie Kennedy," I said.

Ruth said, "She probably recognized you from doing the 'Co-Op'!"

33

ONE FOR THE GIPPER

An alarm's getting louder in the back of my mind. So here goes; I said, "Mr. President, can you hear me?"

I did the weather on the *CBS Morning News* and *CBS This Morning*, filling in for McEwen

I did the weather on CBS for an entire week, and they called me back for a second week when McEwen went on vacation again.

This was about the same time long-time anchor and Arizona TV news legend Bill Close was getting ready to retire, and one day, news director Dave Howell called me into his office. He asked if I would replace Close at anchoring the noon and 5:00 p.m. news. I accepted and got a promotion and a fat raise. My work on CBS may have had something to do with this, and I was happy to do it.

John Goodman, the CBS senior producer, called asking me to do the weather again on CBS, but I told him the good news, that I was leaving weather to become a news anchor. He congratulated me and said, "I guess we can't use you anymore, now that you're a big-time anchor."

Now I was a news anchor, I anchored the noon and 5:00 p.m. news with Claren Scott for a long time. Our five o'clock news was number one, and it led the nation in delivering one of the largest audience shares to the *CBS Evening News*. Claren was bright, beautiful, and a consummate journalist.

Susan Taylor and I anchored for a while on the noon news, and she was a crack-up. There were times after the show that she would throw me down on the set behind the anchor desk, falling to the floor as she yelled, "Let's leg-wrestle!"

Also, many times, there were guests on our noon news who were promoting a charity. And she would say on the air, "Well, Rick and I would love to contribute to your charity."

■ ■ ■

And here's a day I'll never forget. About fifteen minutes before anchoring the noon news, I was in the makeup room, and the producer frantically walked in and asked if I was ready, which I thought was a little unusual, because they never do that.

"Are you ready for the interview with the president?" he asked.

"What president?" I asked.

"The president of the United States!" he exclaimed.

"Ronald Reagan?"

"Yes, he's on our show!"

"Oh my God, no one told me!" This is not unusual in TV news.

Reagan was getting ready to leave the White House, and he had just come out with his memoir, called *An American Life*. He and his wife, Nancy, spent a lot of time in Phoenix visiting his mother-in-law, who at the time lived in the Biltmore area. The president wanted to be on our show to publicize his new book. Perhaps he had watched and liked us. I like to think that, anyway.

My coanchor, Susan Taylor, and I would do the interview, and he would be with us via satellite. Here's how I remember what happened.

We were live on the air, and I was reading the teleprompter. "President Ronald Reagan joins us now live from the western White House in Santa Barbara, California, to talk about his new book, *An American Life*."

Susan and I turned to look in the big TV screen behind us. There was an almost full-face live video of the president, and he was grimacing, with a very uncomfortable look on his face. I knew something was wrong!

"Thank you for joining us on Channel Ten News," I said. He was looking dumbfounded, and that alarm started going off in the back of my mind again. I looked at Susan; she had a look of terror on her face. I turned back to the president and said, "Mr. President, what can we learn about you in your new book that we don't already know about you?"

He was still grimacing and now pointing to his ear. An alarm was getting louder in the back of my mind. So here goes; I said, "Mr. President, can you hear me?"

"Well"—the famous Reagan well—"all I can hear is a loud, confounded buzz in my ear!" he complained.

I looked at Susan, she looked at me, and I looked into the camera and said, "We'll be back in just a moment." (I learned that from Harry Smith.)

Whoever was responsible for this, I don't know, but he or she never got the circuit connected so the president could hear us. It was terrible. During the commercial break, they jerry-rigged a system so he could hear our questions.

I don't remember all that happened after that except for this: I asked, "What's the best thing you've ever done?"

He said, "Well, meeting and falling in love with Nancy, and having her in my life, is more than I ever hoped or dreamed it could be."

The leader of the free world, the man who brought down the Iron Curtain and ended the Cold War, and what was the best thing he'd ever done? Falling in love with his wife. What a man!

34

FOX

"Move over, Dan Rather"—you saw a picture of
Dan Rather—"and make way for Bart Simpson."
Then you saw a picture of Bart.

There were some tumultuous times in which Channel 10 (KTSP and later
KSAZ) and Phoenix television—and, I might add, a bunch of other stations and other cities across the country—were plunged into television
chaos.

During my time at Channel 10, the station was sold a number of times.
One of the last owners was the New York investor Ron Perlman, who also
owns Revlon, the cosmetics company. He fancied himself a would-be media magnate; bought a bunch of stations, including Channel 10; and made
an agreement in 1994 with News Corp's Rupert Murdoch to change its
network affiliation to Fox. Perlman later sold his TV stations, including
Channel 10, to News Corp, which later became Twenty-First Century Fox.

While this was happening, we got a new news director. Tom Dolan
came to us from ABC, and he was a very professional, no-nonsense, hardworking guy. He had a lot of experience running major ABC newsrooms
in San Francisco, Chicago, Philadelphia, and New York.

On his first week on the job, he took me out to dinner. At the time, I was anchoring the noon and five o'clock newscasts. I had no idea what to expect. He ordered a bottle of wine, looked me straight in the eyes, and said, "You are the new business editor!" I was shocked.

I was thinking, *Business editor? What the hell is that?*

Dolan continued, "You'll be the reporter, anchor, and expert on all things business, the economy, and finance." He then laid out what I'd be doing. I had never done anything like this before. I looked him calmly in the eyes, remembering I always wanted to be management's go-to guy when it came to doing new things, and said, "Wow, this is exciting. I'd love to do it." The fact of the matter was, I was scared and apprehensive, but I embraced it and then came to love every second of it.

Dolan later held a full staff meeting to describe the changes he was making. He made a long speech to the entire news department, outlining the new direction Channel 10 would be taking. When it came to me and my new duties, he said, "In addition to anchoring the five o'clock news, Rick D'Amico will become the new business editor and economics reporter and anchor. Rick has the unique talent and ability to take complicated issues and stories and make them easy to understand." He was bragging about me in front of the entire news staff. I felt good.

I anchored a morning show, the noon show, the 5:00 p.m. newscast; wrote, reported, and anchored an evening business report on the 6:00 p.m. news; did a business report on the 9:00 p.m. news three days a week; and did a personal-finance report on the Sunday evening newscast. I was working my butt off, and I loved every second of it. I liked Dolan very much, because he respected people who worked hard and were willing to learn.

My schedule was so severe that he eased up on me and took me off the morning and noon shows, and he hired a producer to help me. She came from the *Arizona Republic*. She had no experience in television and came to be known around the station as "the producer from hell."

One day, I walked into our office, and she was screaming into the phone every four-letter word I'd ever heard and some that were new to me. "And you can go fuck yourself!" she yelled as she slammed down the phone and almost broke it off the cradle.

"Who were you talking to?" I asked.

She yelled, "The fucking governor's office!"

She was abusive to everyone, including me. All the contacts and relationships I'd developed with business leaders in the valley were drying up. They were scared to death of her.

Each time I complained to Dolan about her, he said she was doing fine. Everyone in the station avoided her; she was scary. The other producers called her "the Evil One." Then, one day, she insulted Dolan in a meeting, and he fired her on the spot. When she told me, I didn't know if I should laugh or cry—I was so happy. It was OK for her to insult other people, but not the boss. It's good to be the king.

The day came when Phoenix television, and many other television stations in cities across the country, plunged into television turmoil. I was working a business story in Chandler, Arizona, and had just interviewed a Safeway Supermarket official about grocery prices when I got a call from the assignment desk. "We're going from CBS to Fox," John Warren, the assignment editor, told me on the phone.

"What?"

"That's right. Your assignment just changed; you're on this story now. It's on every newscast. It's the day's big story."

Perlman had cut a deal with Murdock, and soon we would be a Fox Television station. I had the lead story on the 5:00, 6:00, and 10:00 p.m. newscasts. My headline was, and was backed up with video, *"Move over, Dan Rather"*—you saw a picture of Dan Rather—*"and make way for Bart Simpson."* Then you saw a picture of Bart.

I thought this was the worst thing that could happen; my career and Channel 10 were doomed. In my story, I interviewed an *East Valley Tribune* television critic, who told me Channel 10 would be off the air in two years, no network to speak of, no news—we could not survive. Whatever happened to him?

The Fox Network at the time was on Channel 15. Channel 15 wanted to become an ABC affiliate, but ABC was on Channel 3. We would no longer be CBS, which went to Channel 5. Channel 3 ended up with no network at all. What a mess. One Sunday, Ruth and I were in church at

Saint Joan of Arc Catholic Church, and Father Larry was ending the Mass. He said, "Go now, and peace be with you. And Rick D'Amico is not going to Channel 5; he's staying at Channel 10!"

So in the interim, we faced a long period when Channel 10 had no network while waiting for the switch to Fox. We aired black-and-white movies in prime time; our ratings plunged from number one to nothing. "Tonight on Channel Ten, *The Invasion of the Body Snatchers*."

The general manager, Ron Bergamo, tried to comfort the staff. In one of his many voice messages, he said, "The train is leaving the station; either get on or the train will leave you behind." And another huge statement he made to comfort the staff: "Don't worry; we're not going to be Fox-Ten or anything like that." Not long after that, security escorted him out of the building; he was gone. I guessed *he* missed the train. And in case you didn't notice, Channel 10 became Fox-10.

Dolan added news, a lot of news, to the schedule: three hours in the morning, an hour at noon, an hour at five, an hour at six, an hour at nine, and an hour at ten. We had nothing else to put on the air, as we had no network. That was why we were all working so hard to make it work.

When Fox came in, my whole world changed. As it turned out, Fox, in my view, was the best thing to happen to local TV and to me. Fox is the only national network and local TV-station operation, I believe, that is truly committed to local news, and it's been the best thing that's ever happened to my career.

Then Dolan's contract was not renewed, and they brought in another news director, Bill Berra, who, on one of his first days on the job, walked into my office and said, "What's all this business shit?" I looked at him and just shrugged my shoulders. He eliminated all business and financial news, and I was back anchoring the noon and 5:00 p.m. newscasts.

Two more general managers had come and gone, and now what was next? Another news director and another morning show.

35

AN ARIZONA MORNING

*I was standing in front of Ground Zero, where
the World Trade Center had stood. The rubble
was still smoldering. Skeletons of buildings were
still standing; some looked like giant waffle
chips leaning against one another.*

"We have President Obama live at 7:00 a.m. to make a statement, and
Diane Ryan [one of our local reporters] is at the press conference; I'll let
you know when," a producer said frantically.

I asked, "Diane Ryan is covering the president?"

"No, she's at the police station covering a shooting."

The execution of the prisoner in the state prison in Florence, Arizona,
was on hold; the Ninth Circuit Court of Appeals in San Francisco had
ordered a stay. Andrea Robinson and I were getting ready to go on the air
at 7:00 a.m. The producer was frantic and talking really quickly.

"They are going to go ahead with the execution."

"They're not going to do it, but they're going to go ahead and move
Troy into the death house." Troy Hayden was our reporter on the scene,
who was scheduled to be a media witness.

I was confused. "So they're going to do the execution?"

"No!"

"But they are going to go ahead anyway." Huh? Three minutes later, the show opened. I looked into the teleprompter and read what it said: "The execution of Jeffery Landrigan is on."

Troy was live in the big TV screen behind us. I said to him, "So, Troy, the execution is on?"

"No, Rick, I don't know where you got that information. It is not on; it is off."

Welcome to the morning show: five and a half hours of live television where anything can happen, and often does. The producer was shouting, "The valve is frozen!"

Andrea and I looked at each other, dumbfounded. I asked, "What the hell is she talking about?"

Another producer told us, "Go to break." It was chaotic, confusing, and the most fun I've ever had.

When things are live, happening now, in the rush to be first and get stuff on the air, that one producer always got frazzled and never gave us the complete story.

"After the second headline, be serious, because the guy had to jump." The frantic producer was rushing in and out of the studio.

I yelled, "Why did he have to jump?"

"Because his house was on fire!" *Oh my God!* I was thinking, *How was I supposed to know that?*

I had five cohosts during the time I did the show, **and** they were all wonderful. Kathleen Bade moved on to San Diego, Illona Carson left for ABC in Houston, Jenn Burgess left the TV business and is an interior designer, Alexis DelChiaro who went on to work in San Diego and Los Angeles, Kristin Anderson who is on the Hallmark Channel, Syleste Rodriguez, and my most current cohost Andrea Robinson.

Andrea Robinson—well, Andrea was my work wife. She is just an angel. She came to work every day with a smile on her face and always, always was bright and happy and positive and gracious. I think the world of her, and I felt the most comfortable sitting next to her doing our show.

Doing this show every morning was a real challenge. I had to be "on" all the time. It can be fun, confusing, and in many cases stressful, but when breaking news happened, we covered it live. In the process, at times, things were kind of hectic, but we were also watching and reporting history in the making—sometimes routine, sometimes happy, and sometimes very frightening and tragic.

At first, September 11, 2001, was a normal morning. But then we got word that a plane had crashed into one of the buildings of the World Trade Center in New York City. *Just another routine day, with some breaking news story to upset what we had planned*, I thought. I was disappointed.

Then, as we were talking about what probably was some stupid, tragic mistake, we took video live from New York, and I saw it happen: an airliner crashed into the second tower of the World Trade Center. I was in total shock. "This is like a Bruce Willis movie," I said. It was surreal, just unbelievable; I could not believe what I was seeing. The United States of America was under attack! This was one of the longest and most depressing days of my career and of my life.

The Fox News Channel took over coverage. I was assigned to put together a wrap-up package of what had happened, in chronological order. The report was to be on a special newscast.

As I was working on the piece, Ruth called. "That plane that went down in Shanksville, Pennsylvania?" she said, crying.

"Yes?"

"It was shot down by an F-sixteen." She was so choked up that I could barely understand her.

"How do you know?"

"Bill's brother was on duty in the Cleveland Center, and they heard the whole thing."

My brother-in-law Bill has a brother who at the time was a supervisor in the Cleveland, Ohio, air traffic control center. The entire staff on duty heard it all—the bullets crashing into the cockpit and the plane going down—and then later was ordered not discuss it.

Afterward, I received a phone call from a viewer who told me his brother was stationed at Offutt Air Force Base in Omaha, Nebraska. The viewer said his brother told him the same thing—that Flight 93 was shot down by USAF F-16s.

At the end of my piece on what happened, I reported this live on the air. To this day, no one has questioned this report or even challenged it. I did get a number of calls from reporters and authors from across the nation who were working on the same information; I told them what I'd heard and what I'd said in my report. It was later reported that Vice President Dick Cheney said the air force was authorized to shoot it down, but later he denied that it was, and the story ended there. I prefer to believe the vice president.

Two months later, I was standing in front of Ground Zero, where the World Trade Center had stood. The rubble was still smoldering. Skeletons of buildings were still standing; some looked like giant waffle chips leaning against one another.

There were cards and letters from children and people from all around the world posted on makeshift fences and walls of buildings. "God bless America!" they said. And I cried when I saw walls and walls of pictures of people missing in the disaster, with notes from loved ones: "Have you seen my daughter/son/wife/husband? If so, please call me."

And there was a smell, a stench, that I never had smelled before; it turned my stomach. I asked an officer, "What's that smell?"

He said, "Burning flesh."

I was in New York for a week, while the Arizona Diamondbacks were in the World Series playing the New York Yankees, seven weeks after the 9/11 attacks. Photographer Tom Fergus and I were assigned to do our morning show out in front of the Fox News Channel on the Avenue of the Americas. Every morning I would stand on the street and broadcast, and the crowds of people passing by treated me like I was some sort of barricade, in their way as they rushed along.

After the show, we would roam around New York City and shoot stories for the following day. There were at least two police officers on every block. They were very friendly and very helpful, and mostly the people I encountered on the street were very nice.

A highlight was visiting the shrine of the all-American pastime, the original Yankee Stadium. Tom shot me getting on the subway, talking to New Yorkers who at first were kind of standoffish and after a few minutes were very friendly. Many volunteered directions and advice for us on places to go see, best restaurants, story ideas, and best places to take pictures. I hated to get off the subway—we were having such a good time.

We arrived in the Bronx, and there it was: Yankee Stadium. My father would have been proud; he loved the Yankees. Security was extremely tight. We asked a police officer where we could go with our credentials. "Anywhere you want," he replied. We went straight to the Yankee dugout.

Tom and I sat on the Yankee bench, and I swear, we didn't say a word to each other for at least five minutes, just taking it in. This is where they all sat. Ruth, Gehrig, DiMaggio, Mantel, Maris, Ford, Rizzuto, Berra... and then Tom left for a couple of minutes and came back.

"Where'd you go?" I asked.

"I wanted to take a leak in the same toilet Babe Ruth used!" he said. We laughed and went on with our story.

Broadcasting that week in New York was one of the most demanding assignments I ever had. All of us Americans were living in a different world—a world that had changed in a matter of hours—and we wondered if our country would ever go back to being as safe and secure as it had seemed before the 9/11 attacks.

■ ■ ■

Doing the morning show on Channel 10 in Phoenix was really a dream come true. Everybody I knew in my business would have given just about anything to do a talk show. I am so blessed and thankful.

Johnny Carson, Mike Douglas, Merv Griffin, and Regis Philbin were all extraordinary talk-show hosts whom I watched religiously. And while I was on the air, to the very end, I could feel their influence on me.

In the midst of all the chaos—the immediacy of breaking news stories, live shots that don't work or are not ready, equipment breaking down, guests who are too nervous to talk, producers yelling in our ears while we were talking on the air—I've always tried to maintain a calmness and a sense of professionalism, even as everything around us seemed to be caving in.

And time seemed to be so important. Three minutes—that was it. "Wrap," they'd yell in our ear while we were in the middle of an interview or event.

For example, one day a magician was on our show doing a couple of really cool magic tricks. He whipped out a deck of cards, fanned them out, and said, "OK, Rick, pick a card, and don't show me what it is."

I pulled out a card, showed it to the camera, and then was shocked to hear in my earpiece the producer in the control booth say, "Wrap!"

I thought, *Now what do I do? Ask the magician to come back in a few weeks with the rest of the trick?*

My mind is all awash with the memories of celebrities who appeared on our show and bizarre moments that happened behind the scenes.

Gracie Slick was in the studio once. I was asking her about the days of Jefferson Airplane and Jefferson Starship. She said, "Drugs were good; they were fantastic!"

I was in total shock. The executive producer ran into the studio giving me the cut signal—you know, waving your flat hand at your throat. She wanted me to end the interview. But then Slick went on to say, "However, drugs killed all my friends."

Then one time, Tommy Chong was wrapping up our interview, and he said, "Go to my website and buy my glass pipes!" I thought I was going to throw up.

I normally didn't get very nervous when doing the show, but this one morning was very special: Nancy Sinatra was on, in the studio, live with me! She was appearing with us to talk about her show at an Indian casino.

I loved—and to this day still love—Frank Sinatra. I listen to his music nearly every day. I've loved him since the days of early rock and roll. When my friends were buying Fats Domino records, I was buying Frank Sinatra records.

We had just gone into a break when a booking producer rushed over to me. "She's in the green room." I was so excited.

I walked in. "Hi, Nancy, I'm Rick D'Amico; I'm going to interview you." I put my arm around her, hugged her, and said, "You know, I just loved your father, and I love you."

She said, "Your producers told me to be here at seven thirty, but we don't go on for another twenty minutes. Why do we have to be here so early?"

Oh my God, I thought, *she's just like her dad!* But when she got on the air with me, she was wonderful.

Deana Martin, Dean Martin's daughter, was appearing in Phoenix and was booked on our show once. I've never had so much fun with a guest. I sang her father's songs with her. Of course I already knew the lyrics.

Another of my singing idols, Tony Bennett, was on our show a number of times. He was so gracious and polite, and of course I was always a nervous wreck.

Alan Thicke was hosting *Pictionary*, a show that was seen across the nation. He asked me to be on his show.

I flew to LA, and a limo driver met me at the airport and whisked me off to "Television City in Hollywood." I took the elevator to the wrong studio, where I saw Adam Arkin playing a banjo. (Arkin played the role of Aaron Shutt on *Chicago Hope* and was in many other TV shows and feature films.) I said, "Is this the *Pictionary* studio?"

"No, downstairs."

I found the right place, and now I was in the *Price Is Right* studio, where *Pictionary* was also taped. Backstage, there were refrigerators, washing machines, and other appliances all over the place. I was onstage, we were taping the show, and one of my team members was Joan Van Ark. I was crazy about her when she was Valene Ewing on *Dallas*! I was so nervous that she put her hand on my knee to calm me down. I was sure she was just being nice, although I did feel a little sexual tension! Our team captain was Adam Corolla. We were up against Mario Van Peebles and his team. We lost; who was going to argue with Mario Van Peebles? It's worth noting that while Mario Van Peebles has this image of a super-tough guy in his movies, he spent our breaks playing games with his daughters backstage. I got in a limo and flew back to Phoenix. Later, Alan Thicke came on our show with me to play a local version of *Pictionary*.

One day, Paula Deen was live with us on the air, and I mentioned that I loved her accent; it reminded me of when I was on radio in Albany, Georgia. Turns out she'd been living there at the time, and she remembered me from my time on Johnny Reb Radio.

Lou Rawls had moved to the valley, and he was a frequent guest on our show. I had played so many of his records in my disc-jockey years that I was just in awe to speak to him in person. He was such a big star, and he was so kind and gracious.

Senator and former presidential candidate Bob Dole was also very gracious and extremely articulate, and we had something in common. When he came back from the war, he was a patient at Percy Jones Hospital in Battle Creek, Michigan, and we reminisced about living in the Cereal City. He said my interview with him was his best.

John McCain would come on our show when he needed us—when he was running for office—but when *we* needed *him*, he never returned our calls. Frankly, we just never seemed to hit it off; he always seemed to make a comment that I thought was cutting me down. Maybe it was just his sense of humor.

Gilbert Gottfried took over the show twice, and we all laughed hysterically. He interrupted Ron's newscast and said, "Are those teeth real?"

I'll never forget the day a young booking producer came to me with a problem. "Fox would like us to book a couple of actors I've never heard of to talk about a collection of movies; should I book these people or just drop it?" She asked. I took the brochure; it was Donald O'Connor and Jayne Russell. I did the interview.

Jerry Mathers, the Beaver, was a guest some fifty years after his hit television show, *Leave It to Beaver*, and he dressed in character, like he did on the show. It was surreal to sit and talk to him.

One morning, I had a poignant interview with Robert Duvall. The topic was how cowboy or Western movies could be sensitive and still a good story.

Paul Rodriguez and I were sitting on set talking live on the air, and I told him I was raised in an Italian family. He screamed in the camera, "He's an imposter; his real name is Jaime Melendez!"

Kurt Warner taught me how to throw a spiral, and he genuinely cheered for me when I did it right.

Kevin Costner always made himself available to plug his movies, and each time I interviewed him, it was just like talking to an old friend. It's almost as though he was shy. He was a very nice and humble guy.

Perhaps the most civil, humble, and polite guests on the show were the professional wrestlers from the WWE, who were quiet and mannerly. Ted Dibiase was so kind and gentle and quiet. A few days later, I watched a WWE show where he was beating the crap out of his opponent with a chair—pounding the guy's head against the stairway of the ring.

Ray Liotta was sitting in our studio being interviewed by Ilona Carson. The interview ended. I was on camera now, and I looked at him and said, "Do I amuse you? Do you think I'm funny; do you think I'm a clown?"

He laughed and said, "That's good!" We did that scene from *Goodfellas* together where he played mobster Henry Hill, and I was doing Joe Pesci— just like in the film. I thought I was pretty good, but I think Liotta was happy to get out of there.

A few months later, I interviewed the real Henry Hill. He said he wasn't proud of his life in the mob, but please, buy his cookbook.

Speaking of the mob, "Big Pussy" Bompensiero walked out on set and sat down to talk with me. The character from the *Sopranos* was played by Vincent Pastore. I hugged him, just as Tony Soprano would, and I said, "Hey! Are you wearing a wire?" He was—and it was one of our microphones! It got a good laugh. In the middle of the interview, he got a phone call from the *Sopranos*' Bobby Bacala, whose real name is Steve Schirripa. All three of us were having a conversation, live on the air, like I was one of the boys in the *Sopranos*.

Nicolas Cage never seemed to get it. Alexis DelChiaro opened the interview by saying we were Italian and talked with our hands. And he said, "I don't talk with my hands." Lighten up, Nicolas (he's Italian, by the way); we were having fun here.

One of those nights I couldn't sleep. Then the next morning, I was in awe. I was sitting next to one of the biggest legends of Hollywood, Mickey Rooney! Then he got in a fight with his wife on the air when she tried to fix his shirt. I was almost gawking at him, because he was talking to me, little Richey from Wickliffe, Ohio.

Shirley McClain wouldn't come out to the studio, because her dog wouldn't walk on our shiny floor. And finally, when she did, a producer had to hold her dog off camera and within sight. McClain would look only at me and answer only my questions; she never looked once at the female anchor, Jenn Burgess.

Fabian met me at a dinner to do an interview. It was like being back in the fifties when he was a teen idol. I told him he was the original teen idol. And he said, "Well, there was Elvis, you know!"

And, oh, the morning when Connie Stevens walked into the studio live on the air and hugged me—was still in awe.

On another occasion, Sugar Ray Leonard got in the ring with me. Well, it was one of those inflatable rings, and we had those huge inflatable boxing gloves on, and I knocked him down—OK, he tripped—and we laughed and laughed.

When I was a teenager growing up in Ohio, I, like most teens across the country, watched *American Bandstand*. What an amazing experience to have Dick Clark on our show. He was such a nice guy, and he played rock-and-roll trivia with us and came back a number of times.

Many times, I had dreamed of being on the *Tonight Show* with Ed McMahon and Doc Severinsen. Doc was a regular on our show and came back a number of times. One morning he was to teach me how to play the trumpet; little did we know the trumpets were props, and we almost blew our brains out.

And Ed McMahon? Walking into the studio one day, he grabbed me and said, "Hey, Rick, you're the weatherman: How come it's raining in Phoenix? I thought this was a desert!"

I was totally shocked. I said, "What are you doing here?"

He answered, "I'm in town to do a book signing, and you will be there." He was so much fun.

One of the most historic days in the history of the United States, and of the world, was July 20, 1969. Neil Armstrong was about to step foot on the moon. At the time, Ruth and I were hunkered down in our apartment on Euclid Avenue in Wickliffe, Ohio. I was holding my breath—what an event. Neil Armstrong was walking on the moon! Fast-forward about twenty years or so. I was in the studio at Channel 10, and I was talking with Neil Armstrong. And, do you know, he was so gracious, he actually asked me questions about the weather—I think to calm me down, because I was in shock! I could hardly breathe.

I also had the honor of sitting down with Chuck Yeager, the first man to fly faster than the speed of sound. General Yeager was so much fun to talk to. I kidded him about Jeana Yeager, one of the two pilots of the *Rutan Voyager* aircraft, which circled the world without landing or refueling. I said to Chuck, "You must be proud of your daughter." Turns out they're not related, but he laughed it off.

Glen Campbell, who lived in Phoenix for a while, was another regular guest. One morning, he was singing his hit "Rhinestone Cowboy" to the end of our show, and the producer mistimed the segment and added an additional couple of minutes, so over and over again, he sang, "Like a Rhinestone Cowboy" until the show ended. I sang with him, and I thought I was pretty good.

Another Phoenix resident was a regular, Alice Cooper; he was always polite and wanted to make a difference in our community by promoting his charity, "the Solid Rock Foundation." He was a good guy and huge star who gave back.

When I was ten or eleven years old, my older sister, Diane, listened to Johnny Mathis records all day long, so I sang along with them, trying to duplicate his voice. One morning, I was shocked to learn the legendary singer would be on our show. I thought, *All those years of singing along with his records and trying to sound like him are paying off!* I told him what a fan I was and how I'd loved his music since I was ten years old.

He asked, "Do you sing, Rick?"

I answered, "No."

Speaking of singing, the Lettermen were the big vocal group when I was a teen. So again fast-forward about thirty-five years, and I was standing there live on the air, singing "When I Fall in Love" with the Lettermen. They wanted to take me on tour, but you know, I had commitments!

Debbie Reynolds was very formal. She seemed to be doing those old Hollywood poses, but what a star. I could tell she liked me; after all, I was the only one on the staff who could sing "Tammy—Tammy—Tammy's in love!"

And Joan Rivers—oh yes, she was always so funny and, might I say, a little risqué. I told her about the time I accidentally stepped on her foot in Las Vegas; she didn't remember.

When Douglas Fairbanks Jr. sat across from me, I welcomed him to the show by saying, "We're so happy to have with us legendary silver-screen actor Douglas Fairbanks Jr. Welcome to the show Mr....Junior." I was a little nervous.

I was talking with George Carlin once, and we were wrapping up the interview, talking mostly about what you can't say on television. I said, "Thanks a lot, George."

He said, "You're welcome, Rick, and remember: if your erection lasts more than four hours, call a physician!"

I thought, *Oh my God, are we still on the air?* Yes, we were.

When I was eleven years old, in 1954, my father took me to the movies to see *20,000 Leagues under the Sea,* starring Kirk Douglas. Driving home, I told my dad how much I loved the movie.

He said, "Someday, son, you'll probably see it on TV." But never in a million years did I suspect that someday I would interview Kirk Douglas. It was a wonderful four minutes with Douglas. I told him about that day with my dad, and he genuinely liked that story.

I had a two-day assignment on a cruise ship, the *Grand Princess,* in New York City. I was there to do our morning show live, and I was standing face-to-face with and interviewing Buzz Aldrin, the second man to walk on the moon. "Do you find it strange that we have more computing power in our laptops today than you had in the entire Apollo Program at the time?" I asked.

"No, we had what it took to get the job done," he replied. He was a tough, no-nonsense guy. I think we hit it off pretty well.

Also on that cruise ship, I talked with Rita Moreno, who followed me around and kept asking me to do another interview. "Hey, Rick, you wanna do another interview? I got so much more to tell you," she said, just in fun.

I also spent time with Bob Keeshan, Captain Kangaroo. I told him his show was the last time CBS was number one in the morning. He was quiet and soft-spoken and very polite.

I also did an interview with six-time Ms. Olympia Cory Everson; at the end of the interview, she kissed me on the cheek. I was in heaven!

I talked with Gavin MacLeod, who played Murray on the *Mary Tyler Moore Show* and Captain Stubing on the *Love Boat*. A couple got married on the boat, and we shot it for a segment; MacLeod cried during the ceremony. Every time we ran into each other on the boat for two days, he always said, "Hi, Rick!" That assignment on the *Grand Princess* was one of my best.

John Glenn, the first American to orbit the earth, the third man in space, and former US senator from Ohio was in the studio with me to be interviewed about his last space trip. He said, "You're from Wickliffe, Ohio? I have great friends there in Lake County."

We reminisced about living in Ohio. He gave me the patch of his final space mission, which I'm looking at now in my office at home.

Sometimes I get involved in a television show and *live* it. I mean, I feel like I know the characters, the emotion, and the drama they are living in the show. One such television series was *Law and Order: SVU*, starring Christopher Meloni and Mariska Hargitay.

Many times during our morning planning meeting, if there was a story about a big court case, like *Jodi Arias* for example, I would pipe in, "Hey, I'm an expert on the justice system; I watch Christopher Meloni on *Law and Order*."

So this is where this is going: Christopher Meloni was a guest on our show, in the studio, on the couch. It was a big deal for me, and I just couldn't resist telling him how I thought he was such a brilliant actor. However, like a lot of famous people in show business and music, I noticed he didn't seem to realize the impact he had on people's lives, or how important he was to us. Maybe that's what makes these actors so good?

One morning, Donald Trump called in to the show. I asked, "Do I call you 'the Donald' or 'Mr. Trump'?"

He said, "You can call me anything you want." He talked for about five minutes. Andrea and I barely got a question in, but we thanked him. At the time, we had not given him much of a chance as president of the United States. Boy, were we wrong.

It was a Saturday night at the WJ Marriott Resort in North Phoenix, and Cory, Andrea, and I were standing onstage. I was the first one to speak, and I looked down at the audience in front of me. There, sitting just a few feet away, were Halle Berry, Kevin Costner, Billy Crystal, Lee Greenwood, Bret Michaels, and Reba McEntire. Mohammed Ali Fight Night was about to get underway, and the audience was loaded with stars from show business, politics, broadcasting, and sports. Later, Reba and Bret said they watched our show all the time, and Bret Michaels eventually came on our show to be a guest.

And then there was perhaps one of the most historical figures in the history of Arizona and in the history of US conservative politics, Barry Goldwater.

Ruth and I were invited to his house for a function for the Arthritis Foundation. I thought we would drop in, have a few drinks, and socialize, and perhaps we would get a glimpse of the former senator and presidential candidate. As we walked up to his front door—walking up a mountain, by the way, in Paradise Valley—there was a man standing at the front door. I thought it might be a butler or a greeter. At first I couldn't make out who he was; then, as we got closer, I saw it was Barry Goldwater!

He welcomed us to his house and gave us a personal tour. He showed us his gun collection and his collection of Native American photographs, which, of course, he'd taken himself. He was an accomplished photographer, which had led him into politics. He even showed us his bedroom!

We talked about his early days as a pioneer in building Phoenix and his hobbies, including ham radio. I asked him, "What's the best thing you've ever done?"

And you know what he said? Moving my wife here from Indiana! What a man.

Hugh Downs has been a long-time resident of Phoenix. When he came out with a book about living in the valley, one of our producers called him and asked if we could do an interview on our show. He replied, "Who will do the interview?"

The producer responded, "Rick D'Amico."

"Send him over," he said. To his house!

Photographer Ken Thorp and I did the interview on his back patio, and when it was over, Hugh Downs's wife, Ruth, brought out a platter of cookies and coffee, and we sat there and talked for over an hour. What a nice man—gentle, gracious, kind, and very bright. I was in awe; I had watched him on TV since I was a child. He was a pioneer in television, as Jack Parr's *Tonight Show* sidekick announcer, host of *Concentration* on NBC, anchor of the *Today Show*, and on ABC's *20/20* with Barbara Walters. He was someone I'd always respected and loved because he was such a bright and articulate man.

A few years later, I was backstage at the annual production of KTAR radio's the *Christmas Carol*. I had a minor role. I saw Hugh Downs sitting in the corner all by himself. Most of the performers there, all members of the local media, paid no attention to him. They were all young and probably had no idea who he was. I sat with him, and we talked about how much broadcasting has changed over the years.

Another exciting morning for me: we got Regis! If there was any one person whom I thought was the very best TV personality of all time, it's without a doubt Regis. I started the interview, "Here's a guy I just love— it's Regis Philbin!"

"I love you too, Rick!" he exclaimed. "Rick! I love you too!"

Regis's mother was Albanese, or Albanian Italian, like my mother; we had a lot in common. Many people today say I'm just like him. I never tried to be; he was just so wonderful on the air, it kind of rubbed off. A few years later, I was interviewing Kelly Ripa, and she was familiar with the story of both our mothers being Albanian Italians. Regis must have told her.

One day, I had just gotten off the air when sports anchor Todd Whitthorne came rushing up to me. "Rick, there's a phone call for you."

I said, "Who is it?"

He said, "I don't know, but believe me, you got to take this call."

I picked up the phone. "Hello, this is Rick D'Amico speaking."

"Rick, it's Johnny Holliday!" Oh my God! My all-time idol, the Cleveland disc jockey whom I had listened to in high school, and the one man who had inspired me to want to be in broadcasting. Todd knew him from the time he worked in Washington, DC, and had him call me. We talked about our business, how crazy it was, and I told him what an inspiration he was to me and my career. This was one of my biggest joys!

After the morning of 9/11, I was exhausted, and for days, I stayed glued to the national coverage. With hardly any sleep at all and stressed out on the job, I would return home and crash on the couch with the Fox News Channel on. At times I would doze off and wake up to the soft, melodious, confident, and calming sound of Mayor Rudy Giuliani conducting a news conference. He immediately became my hero. His calming influence on the nation's and New York's tragedy was miraculous and I believe helped people to cope.

Well, can you imagine my excitement to learn, some years later, that he was going stop by our studios to be on our show? I was so honored to interview Rudy Giuliani. He was such a gentleman and so thoughtful and sincere. After the interview, during a commercial break, I told him I was so proud he was Italian. He grabbed me in a big bear hug. How great that was!

By this time I had finally connected with one of the finest ear, nose, and throat doctors in the country, Dr. Jeffery McKenna. We call him the "Rock Doc." He is the go-to doctor when stars come into town to perform. His office is adorned with many autographed pictures of very famous people, from the Rolling Stones to Barbra Streisand, and yours truly. After a number of examinations, he told me, "You have an abnormality in your vocal chords. Somewhere along the line, you probably got a virus, and your vocal chords changed and thickened." This is what had made my voice lower and more suitable for broadcasting—another one of those miracles in my career!

I've talked, met, and had fun with so many famous people from all walks of life, including show business and politics, from local and national to international stars. I could never begin to list them all; it's all been so wonderful and so exciting. Never in a million years did I ever dream that I, a blue-collar guy from Wickliffe, Ohio, would have had such a wonderful career!

But more important than all the celebrities I've had the pleasure to meet and interview, the real treasure of my career has been meeting the people who have accepted me into their homes every morning—our audience. Many of these people consider me one of the family and, as many whom I have met along the way have said, a real friend.

This was and is the true treasure of my career!

36

JUST A ROUTINE DAY

I was doing my usual complaining about how tough my life is. "Well, why don't you shave her legs tonight? That ought to be fun!"

And then there was just the routine of showing up for work every day, five days a week, for three, four, and sometimes five hours a day on the air trying to be glib, happy, knowledgeable, and bright. It's impossible; we all know that, but we try.

I've always compared my job to cramming for a final exam—every day. And honestly, no one, except those who do it, really knows what it takes to do a TV morning-news show. Most people think you show up and have fun, with no effort, and just goof around. To do this type of show takes a lot of hard work.

This was my typical day. At 4:00 a.m., my iPhone alarm would go off. I would sit up in bed, flip on the light, and check the e-mail alerts on my phone. Then my second alarm would go off, the one on my clock radio. I would turn on the TV and put the Fox News Channel on loud, so I could hear the news while I was getting ready. I needed to be informed; who knew what topic would come up on the show?

After showering and getting dressed, I would go downstairs, where Ruth was fixing me breakfast. I would read three papers before leaving for work: the *Arizona Republic*, *USA Today*, and the *Wall Street Journal*.

Then, driving to work, I would listen to KTAR Radio and the morning news; check in for their sports report; and also try to figure out what was on the mind of Beth McDonald from KEZ, who was featured on our show three times in the morning. Doing those live segments with Beth was one of the highlights of the morning, and I enjoyed every second with her.

I would arrive in the newsroom at about 6:00 a.m. I'd go to my desk and sign on the computer to check the National Weather Service webpage for my weather briefing. Then I would scan the news websites and the Associated Press for headlines. The executive producer would give me a briefing at 6:20 a.m. These were mostly confusing, as she spoke in incomplete sentences, so I always conferred with my cohost, Andrea, to get clarification. And most times Andrea wasn't told what was on the show! Then I was off to makeup. I was in place for the 7:00 a.m. hour at 6:40, and I was listening to Cory McCloskey's weathercast, to make sure we were both on the same page.

Cory McCloskey is a genius. I have never, in all my fifty-plus years of working in broadcasting, met or worked with anyone more entertaining. And looking back at all the places and stations and people I've worked with, that says a lot. Cory just lights up the show. No one I meet can say enough good things about him and how much they love him. Here's a typical comment I received on Facebook one day: "OMG, would you tell Cory I absolutely love him? I turned on the TV this morning, and in a split second he had me choking on my coffee laughing when he fell on the floor looking up at the stadium ceiling! You guys are very lucky working with such a character." Our morning show was so lucky to have him.

At 6:50 I would be on the air. I would introduce Beth McDonald, and the entire exchange would be totally off-the-cuff and usually hilarious.

"My wife really ticked me off yesterday," I might say.

"Oh really, what happened?" Beth would have that mischievous look on her face.

"Well, while sitting out on the patio last night, she told me how much she loves my razor, and she said she used it to shave her legs!" I was doing my usual complaining about how tough my life is.

"Well, why don't you shave her legs tonight? That ought to be fun!" *Oh my God, we're in trouble again,* I thought.

We're all sitting on the couch, Alexis DelChiaro might start laughing, and it would take at least ten minutes to get her to stop. She was an amazing personality who just lit up the screen and any room she happened to be in.

In the middle of a conversation about traffic on one of our freeways, Syleste Rodriguez would butt in and say she had GE appliances! She was off the wall and so funny. If anyone has a smile that can warm the hardest of hearts, or just light up a room, it is Syleste. I came to know her well, and I miss her.

Kristin Anderson would sit quietly and pat her hair and then look at me and say, "I don't get your jokes!" Some people have a God-given talent so warm and genuine it blows you away—that's Kristin. She's an electrifying, beautiful, extremely happy, outrageous personality, who was just a joy to work with. She's like me, kind of crazy and outspoken. We've had many conversations about management not getting us. She has the presence of a morning-show personality you would see in Los Angeles, New York, or Chicago or on a national show. And, that's where she is now—one of the hosts of Hallmark channel's *Home and Family*.

And Ron Hoon. Ron was always the Rock. He is a consummate journalist and historian. When he came on our show, I quickly realized he was just what we needed to add credibility to what we did. He's the best at what he does. (Although, come on, those ties! They're terrible!)

And our reporters were so amazing. Diane Ryan; Alexis Vance; Liz Kotalik, who I just barely got to know; Courtney Griffin, who is such a nice person; and Anita Roman are the best you'll find anywhere on morning television. I was amazed when they would appear on camera to cover all the breaking news of the morning, many times rushing to the scene of a story with little or no advance information—can you imagine? They did it with such poise and credibility.

For the next three hours, anything could happen. Who knew? Riots in the Middle East, illegals running from a drop house, a NASA liftoff, the Academy Awards, a movie star who was next to be interviewed, followed by a doctor to talk about the latest cure for some disease. Donald Trump running for president. Then, after all this, I would try to talk intelligently about what was going to happen with the weather, while the sheriff of Pinal County was up next in our studio to talk about illegal immigration and drug trafficking, followed by a break and the latest poll on politics, followed by what had happened the night before on a Fox show or *American Idol*. Then the wars in the Middle East or a tsunami in Japan. Or Osama Bin Laden was killed. Or coverage on the civil war in Syria. Who could keep up with all this?

Truly, it's the producers who made the show. They are the hardest-working people in the newsroom and are the true journalists who write the show, schedule the guests, assemble the segments, and make sure everything gets on and off on time. They deserve much more credit and, I might add, much more pay than they get.

Producer Jenn Doan is the most remarkable person behind the scenes. She produced the 8:00 a.m. and 9:00 a.m. hours, and she is the hardest-working person I've ever met in broadcasting. Jenn, as a baby, was one of the original Vietnam boat people, part of the mass exodus of the Vietnamese to other lands at the end of the Vietnam War. Her family found their way to Oklahoma. She attended the University of Oklahoma and ultimately became an associate producer at Channel 10. She has the most amazing work ethic. She worked so hard that she was promoted to producer of the 8:00 and 9:00 a.m. hours and is outstanding! I have watched her set up a show, run the cables, set up the equipment, write the show, monitor the show while it's on the air, and comfort us when things go wrong. I couldn't have worked without her.

The one person who tried to hold the show together and keep it focused was our executive producer, Mary Morse Vasquez. It was a tough job and many times she had difficulty communicating when all hell was breaking loose. I think she always thought I could read her mind, but afterward, when it all calmed down after the show, we would laugh and say we would try again the next day.

In an earlier chapter, I mentioned the one man who was in charge, the vice president of news, Doug Bannard. He had such a talent of choosing just the right people to work with, and it resulted in a loving group of people who were like family. I know I must have given him and Mary a lot of headaches, and I was thankful they were so professional in handling such a hotheaded anchor—me!

I would be off the air at ten. Coming off an adrenalin rush, I would be emotionally drained. Have you ever seen the end of a sports event, such as a baseball game, when the team did well and they're all jumping up and down celebrating? That's what it feels like for the talent when the show ends. But, as we walked into the newsroom after the show, no one would say anything—just quiet.

Then I would write the next day's "News of the Weird" feature immediately while scanning the Internet for show ideas.

After that, we'd have an agonizing meeting at ten thirty to discuss what was to be on the show the following day, which never seemed to happen the following day.

Then we would shoot promos for the next day's show, and I would anchor the noon news.

By the time twelve thirty rolled around, I would be pooped; I would sit at my desk and wait until about 1:30 p.m. Then I was out the door, and I would drive straight home, of course listening to news radio to find comments for the following day's show.

I would turn on the Fox News Channel, listening to what was happening while I was getting into my around-the-house clothes.

I tried to watch all the evening newscasts, have dinner, then sit out on the patio and prepare for the next day's show. A three-minute interview with a Hollywood movie star or a politician, or whomever, usually takes about an hour of preparation. Many times a producer will give you a book and say, "This person is going to be on our show tomorrow." I would begin to read that and try to figure out what questions I was going to ask.

And Fox loved us to interview the stars of their TV shows. So we would watch the shows. When *X Factor* or *American Idol* was on, it was usually two and sometimes three days a week, and some shows are two hours long.

To do this show, you have to know a little something about everything— I mean everything!

Actually, cramming for a final exam is a lot easier.

37

SURVIVAL

I had to stand out, be a personality, be outra-
geous! I didn't want to be one of the TV gasbags
who read other people's words and get a feeling
of celebrity for just being on camera.

Thirty years! Thirty years at one TV station. Thirty years at any job nowa-
days is unheard of. The station changed ownership at least five times;
there have been seven general managers and five news directors. And
through this time, my career certainly had its ups and downs.

New members of management always want to change things. I decid-
ed that, to survive, I had to suck it up, set my ego aside, and just do my job.
There were many days where this was extremely tough for me; many days,
I was on the edge of just walking out and chucking the whole career. Joel
Osteen, pastor of Lakewood Church in Houston, Texas, whose TV pro-
gram I watch regularly, said, and I quote, "Bloom where you are planted!"
I had to keep this in mind every day.

For example, there was a time when, after being promoted to anchor
of the morning show, I was pushed aside. My role was diminished, demoted. The promise from my boss was broken. I was excluded from the promos and completely ignored. It was a tough time, and I thought seriously

about quitting. During those dark days, I was hidden in a back studio while coanchors were doing the news in the big studio. They would toss to me for a second, and I would try to say something funny and toss back to them; it was awful.

But I remembered my history—for example, I considered that lunch with newsman Bob Engle in Cleveland, Ohio, when I was just starting out, when he'd told me it's about talent. And I remembered all those jobs of my past where I'd been hired because of my talent.

I decided that to survive, I had to stand out, be a personality, be outrageous! I didn't want to be one of those TV gasbags who read other people's words and get a feeling of celebrity for just being on camera.

So I did everything to make myself visible on the show, cracking jokes and making fun of the anchors. I thought up crazy things like "On This Day in History," which I resurrected from my radio days and made into a comedy bit; "The Thought of the Day"; and the most famous and well-liked segment I did, called "News of the Weird."

"The Thought of the Day" and "News of the Weird" became staples on the show, getting the highest ratings, and survived throughout the years. After retiring, I was swamped with people on Facebook and Twitter demanding I continue with "Thought of Day" and "News of the Weird."

Little by little, perhaps because of my craziness and because I was so outspoken, and perhaps because of my talent, after about eight years, I got to do what I was originally promised—be a cohost of the show.

For the longest time, we were told to shut up, not to ad-lib. I would start talking, and the producer in the booth would tell me to wrap. Then, Beth McDonald came on our show, joining us live from her radio studio at KEZ Radio, and everything changed.

Beth and I would just chat—have a conversation. We were talking about our lives, our spouses, our children, doing the dishes, wearing pantyhose—just about living. And the ratings went up. After that, the management allowed us to talk, to engage in conversation, and the ratings continued to climb. We finally became number one. It took at least ten years for management to figure this out. Conversation about our lives makes for good morning television—something I knew from my very first days in broadcasting some forty years earlier.

The comments I got from our audience, whether they were from Facebook, Twitter, voice mail, e-mail, or in person, were always the same: "I love you because you're so real, and you have so much fun." Never does anyone say, "I love your news," or "I love the coverage you give to crime, or health, or whatever!" It's always, "You're like family to me." I believe that's the best comment you can get from your audience.

And, of course, it's the people I've worked with over the years who have made all this possible. The photogs (news photographers), tape editors, production crew who manned the cameras and directed the show, and the amazing broadcast engineers—they all became family, and each and every one of them was a joy to work with.

38

AM I LUCKY?

Fifty years after my first day in speech class, I stood in the banquet room of Pine Ridge Country Club in Wickliffe, Ohio. I was being inducted into the Wickliffe High School Hall of Fame.

One day, I got a call from a man in Chandler, Arizona. "Hey, Rick," he said. "I'm from Cleveland, and you and I graduated from high school about the same time. I, like you, listened to all the big radio DJs in Cleveland, at the time, and I wanted to be in broadcasting, just like you. Do you suppose we were listening to the same DJs at the same time living in different parts of the city?" He went on talking about how much he loved broadcasting, how he wanted to be on the air; it was his dream.

"What do you do?" I asked.

He said, "Work in a grocery store."

"Did you ever work in broadcasting?" I asked.

He answered, "I tried it, but it didn't work out."

We hung up and I thought, *Me too. I tried it, and it didn't work out.* All those jobs in radio, fifteen jobs in nineteen years, moving everywhere; the TV stations, with crazy, paranoid, vindictive people, and all those management crazies—I tried it, a whole bunch of times, and it didn't work out.

It was never about the money or being a star; it was just what I wanted to do, so I kept on doing what I loved.

One day I was standing in line inside a gas station, and a truck driver was loading bottles on some shelves in the back of the store.

When it came to be my turn at the cash register, I said, "I would like four Powerball tickets, please."

The driver in the back of the store said, "Rick D'Amico? What do you need Powerball tickets for?"

I looked at him, dumbfounded. "You know? To get rich?"

He replied, "With your luck, you'll probably win!"

Am I lucky? After reading all this, what do you think? My career tells the story of just plain hard work and plenty of heartache.

I was born in Cleveland, Ohio, to a poor family in 1944. My father, Joseph Michael D'Amico, was a loving Italian family man who worked in a factory, overnight, the graveyard shift. My mom and dad; my sister, Diane; my brother, Dennis; and I lived in a housing project east of Cleveland. We had no money; my mother used to tell me my father came home with his paycheck every other week, and it was seventy-five dollars.

He saved enough money to put a down payment of a couple hundred dollars on a house. The entire cost of the house was $10,000.

My mother never worked and never knew how to drive a car. One Sunday morning, October 9, 1956, my father was out in the backyard cutting the grass when he suddenly keeled over and died of a heart attack. I was twelve years old. After that, we had no money and no insurance; we lost our house and had to move to an apartment in Wickliffe, Ohio.

My mother got a job working in a restaurant. I remember days when she was ecstatic that she got a ten-cent-an-hour raise!

She wasn't home when I left for school in the morning, and she wasn't home when I came home. I was alone and on my own, so I hung around with guys who were perhaps not good for me. One day, coming out of the movies, two of my so-called friends and I were walking through a parking lot, and we discovered a car with the keys in it. We took it for a joyride. The cops picked us up and threw us in jail, and we got probation. I was a bad kid. My mother prayed and prayed for me to turn around.

She transferred me over to Wickliffe High School, and this is where my life changed.

On my first day in speech class, I met Michael Lenenski, the speech teacher. I announced to the class that I was taking the class because I dreamed of being in broadcasting. Lenenski took me under his wing and got me involved in speech, dramatics, choir, and announcing on the PA system.

From that day on, I was on my way. I had no money for college, so I joined the air force. You know the rest.

On August 19, 2010, fifty years after my first day in speech class, I stood in the banquet room of the Pine Ridge Country Club in Wickliffe, Ohio. I was being inducted into the Wickliffe High School Hall of Fame. Mr. Lenenski was in the audience, and I acknowledged him for turning my life around. It was a proud moment for me and for him. It was a much bigger honor than receiving the Emmy Award, the Silver Circle Award from the Television Academy of Arts and Sciences, and all the other awards I've gotten in the past.

So am I lucky? I don't think so. Success came to me because I was willing to pay the price—work hard, but have fun.

But if I am lucky, it's beyond a doubt because I had a wonderful mother. Through all the bad times and good times, she would grab me, throw her arms around me, plant huge kisses on my face, and say, "Richey, I love you, I just love you!" She had no education but was the most loving and positive person I have ever known. Many times, when I doubted my abilities to announce the band at a football game in high school or go on the air in Cleveland, Ohio, she would encourage me, saying, "You're just wonderful, son; you have the brightest, most wonderful personality, and you have a talent from the Lord. You will always do well. I love you, son; I just love you!"

My mother went on to live with the Lord on July 26, 2012, at the age of ninety-eight. During the visiting hours at Orlando-Donsante Funeral

Home, Michael Lenenski, my high-school speech teacher, came to pay his respects, along with Lou Massey, my old buddy from WREO in Ashtabula. My high-school buddies Tim Reid and Joe Siciliano came to support my family too, as did neighbors from the time we lived in the housing project where I was born. My mom loved everyone she met, and it showed that night.

39

MY LITTLE SECRET

And here's my little secret: me too!

I never considered myself a journalist, a DJ, or a news anchor; my mission throughout my career was to be a broadcaster. I believe a broadcaster is a member of the community who serves its best interests. If what I have done over the years has served to enlighten, inform, and help make someone's life better and, hopefully, happier, I consider my career worthwhile. And to think it all started when I was about twelve or thirteen years old, in my bedroom.

Saturday mornings were special to me. While all my friends were out playing baseball or football, I was locked up in my room, in my make-believe radio studio, doing radio shows. It was a form of play.

I don't know if any of my high-school friends went on to play football or baseball for a living, but you know what? I went on to play broadcasting for a living, for more than fifty years. It was never about the money, prestige, or celebrity. It was just about doing what I wanted to do and loved to do, a form of play.

I had lunch with Tim Reid, one of my high-school buddies who went on to become a successful attorney in Cleveland, Ohio, when he visited Phoenix one day. We reminisced, and Tim told me something I'll never forget. "You know, Rich," he said, "you were the only one in our senior class who went on to do what you said you were going to do—the only one who followed his dream and achieved it!" Tim was the one who nominated me for our school's hall of fame. Thanks, Tim!

■ ■ ■

John Chancellor was a well-known TV news anchor who spent most of his career with NBC News. He anchored *NBC Nightly News* from 1970 to 1982.

I happened to catch his last day on NBC in, I believe, July 1993. At the end of the broadcast, Chancellor reminisced about his storied career, the good and bad times covering stories around the world, and how much he loved his job.

Then he said, "And you know what? Here's a little secret: I would have done it all for free."

And here's my little secret: me too!

CPSIA information can be obtained
at www.ICGtesting.com
Printed in the USA
FSOW03n1142280217
31370FS